PROMISE
POINT

PROMISE POINT

GOD'S HOPE
A FAMILY RESTORED

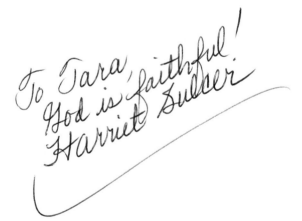

HARRIET SULCER

LOOKING GLASS BOOKS

Published by
Looking Glass Books, Inc.
Distributed by John F. Blair, Publisher

Copyright © 2015 by Harriet Sulcer
Written in collaboration with Dick Parker
Cover photograph copyright © 2015 Brinley Harris
Jacket design by Burtch Hunter Design

Unless otherwise noted, all Scripture quotations are taken from the Holy Bible, New International Version®, NIV® Copyright © 1973, 1978, 1984, 2011 by Biblica, Inc.® Used by permission. All rights reserved worldwide.

Scripture quotations marked NASB are taken from the New American Standard Bible®. Copyright © The Lockman Foundation 1960, 1962, 1963, 1968, 1971, 1972, 1973, 1975, 1977, 1995 by the Lockman Foundation.

Scripture quotations marked AMP from the Amplified Bible. Copyright © The Lockman Foundation 1954, 1958, 1962, 1964, 1965, 1987.

Scriptures marked KJV are taken from the King James Version of the Bible.

Give Thanks, by Henry Smith, Copyright © 1978 Integrity's Hosanna! Music. All rights reserved. Used by permission.

ISBN 978-1-929619-58-0

Manufactured in Canada

For Lou, with all my love.
We finished very well, didn't we?

For our children, Christy and Barry, Andrea and Jerry,
and Kevin and Brittany,
and our grandchildren, Brittan and Adam, Aiden, Hudson, Brinley,
Alden, Maleah, Addison, Tristan, and Dylan.

For my parents,
Peter and Harriet Stovall, our beloved Mimi and Poppy,
who provided a loving home and a godly legacy.

And for our Heavenly Father, the Author of our story.

CONTENTS

The Lord Is Here: *Jehovah-shammah*   1
  Falling into Darkness   3
  Tax Notices in the Descending Darkness   4
  A Glimmer of Light   6
  Into Your Hand   11
  My Daughters' Strength   12
  Be Still and Know   13
  Financial Rock Bottom   16
  No Mercy   19

The Lord My Shepherd: *Jehovah-raah*   21
  Strike Your Match!   23
  Father and Son   24
  My Father's Dreams for Me   26
  Part of the Family   28
  Hope and a Future   31
  Love, Death, and a Challenge   34
  "Trust Me"   36
  Passages   36
  The Crusade House   38
  Lou and I Make a Promise   38
  In Vietnam: Under the Shadow of the Almighty   40
  A Miracle Worker   45
  Super Lou   46
  The Most Bittersweet of Times   48
  The Gift of a Son   48
  At Home for Sunday Dinner   49
  Growing . . . Apart   51
  Priorities   52
  To the Farm   52
  Oh, Lord, Is This What You Want?   55
  Sleeping in the Car   58
  Pebbles for Goats   59
  At Home in the Woods   59
  Encouragers, Just in Time   61

Honeysuckle Dreams 63
Snow Days! 66
A Young Evangelist 67
Children First. Always. 68
Mimi, a Tree Climber 70
Hard Times in Mississippi 71
Total Commitment 73
Unconditional Love Will Break Through 79
The Beginning of Lou's Journey 84
New Product, Lost Sales 85
Isolated in the Congregation 85

The Lord My Healer: *Jehovah-rapha* 87
Unspoken Prayer . . . Answered 89
Exchanging My Life for His Life in Me 89
Kevin and Lou Connect in Canada 90
Completely Forgiven, Fully Accepted 93
Set Free! 96
Going Public 100
Kevin's Prodigal Journey 102
Another Lost Son 104
Always Connected 105
Building a Business from the Basement 106
Living on Oatmeal 108
A Letter Home 110
My Brother's Short Visit 110
A River in the Desert 111
Bright Hope for Tomorrow 112
Prayers of My Sons-in-Law 116
A Side Road in Lou's Journey 116
A Home for Me 117
Praying God's Word 120
Glimmers of Hope 121
New Year's Day Prayer for Faith 121
A Vision of Kevin's Future 124
A Particular Time and Place 126
Prayers of Samaritan's Purse 127
Communion with the Lover of My Heart 129
A Jericho Walk 133

The Lord My Peace: *Jehovah-shalom*   137

  Blood-N-Fire   139
  A New Creation   142
  Coming Home: Not Like in the Movies   143
  A Supernatural Love   148
  A Wedding, a New House, and Reconciliation   150
  Can the Kids Come Over?   153
  Complete Reconciliation: Kevin and Lou   154
  Cody   155
  Unfinished Business   156
  God Knocks Down the Walls of Isolation   161
  Lou's Love Language   168
  Promise Point   171
  Canoe Adventure   173
  Becoming a Person of Influence   174
  The Influence of a Father   177
  A Grandfather's Powerful Influence   179
  Going Fishing   181
  Precious Days   183
  Sunrise   187
  Hope in God's Faithfulness   189

A NOTE ON THE CONTENTS TITLES

While on my journey, I followed a study by Kay Arthur on the names of God, and I began to see the many ways the Lord was revealing Himself to me. He became my Shepherd, my Healer, my Peace, and so much more. And He was always with me, every moment of every day.

I waited patiently for the LORD;
    And He inclined to me and heard my cry.
He brought me up out of the pit of destruction,
    out of the miry clay,
And He set my feet upon a rock
    making my footsteps firm.
He put a new song in my mouth,
    a song of praise to our God;
Many will see and fear
    And will trust in the LORD.
                    —Psalm 40:1–3, NASB

THE LORD IS HERE

Jehovah-shammah

*The worst thing that happened to my family and me became
the best thing that ever happened to us. What the world
called a breakdown became my spiritual breakthrough—
the defining point in my life. God was there at every moment.*

1991

Falling into Darkness

MY DAUGHTER Christy came to my hospital room and said the doctors wanted to move me to the psychiatric ward. I was as broken as a person could be, and their only hope for me was long-term psychiatric treatment.

For months I had been trying to hold everything together—to maintain the illusion that my life was just fine. My husband had left us ten months earlier, but I didn't tell anybody except my closest friends. If I don't tell anybody, I thought, maybe Lou will come home before they find out.

Our son, Kevin, who had just finished his junior year in high school, was sinking fast into a mire of alcohol and drugs, and I had no idea how to help him.

Our finances were in shambles. We were in the process of declaring bankruptcy and losing our house to foreclosure.

I'd lost my husband, my son, my financial security, and my home. Now I was losing all hope, plunging into the deepest darkness I had ever experienced—falling and falling.

Christy came over to the bed, took my hand, and said, "Mom, they cannot help you here. What you have is a spiritual problem, not a mental problem. You're in the hospital because you've tried to fix everything. The bottom line is, you can't fix any of it. You can't fix Daddy, you can't fix Kevin, you can't fix your finances overnight, you can't save the house. It's just a house. You have to walk away from it. We want you to work on fixing you, and only God can do that."

I was listening, but I must have glazed over, because Christy spoke very plainly, like she was talking to a child or an old, old woman. My life and our family were so shattered, only God could repair them. I was so broken, I couldn't comprehend how broken I was.

"I'm going to sign you out of the hospital," Christy said. "And I have to tell you, your doctor is very upset with me. He doesn't want me to take you. But I'm twenty-two, and I can do this. Andrea and I are taking you home. God is going to get you well again."

"Okay," I whispered. "Take me home."

So they signed me out, put me in a wheelchair, and rolled me to the car. On that day, I became the child, Christy became the mother, and God became my Healer.

This book is my account of His amazing work in our lives.

Tax Notices in the Descending Darkness

BEFORE MY breakdown I had been trying to hold on to my son, persuade my husband to come back home, and create enough income to dig our way out of debt. My business was my only flicker of success. NSA was a direct-sales company that sold water filters and air filters, and three years earlier I had built a team of distributors, including homebuilders and veterinarians. They grew and sustained their own markets, and during that time my family experienced our best years financially.

Then the company changed its product line to Juice Plus, a whole-food-based nutrition supplement. Many of my sales team did not follow the transition, and my revenue dropped by two-thirds overnight. Anyone could see the long-term upside to the product change, but I couldn't build my Juice Plus team fast enough to meet our financial obligations.

In the midst of building the new team, I opened my mailbox and found notices from the Internal Revenue Service and the Georgia Department of Revenue in quick succession. The return addresses alone frightened me. I was the student who always turned in her homework on time. The idea of trouble with the IRS was beyond anything I could imagine. I began to tremble when I read that we hadn't paid taxes for several years—the years when the income from my business had been at its highest—and they were demanding payment at once. Surely this was a mistake.

I immediately called our friend Carey Barnes, an accountant. Carey was a high school friend of Lou's, and his wife, Sheila, had been my prayer partner for years. I took the notices to Carey's office so he could straighten it out, but there was no mistake. We owed the money. Lou had started his career as a banker and had always managed our personal and business finances, but in the years leading up to our separation, he had experienced several major health crises and, I believe now, depression. Our marriage was falling apart, and we weren't talking to each other about anything but our children—not our marriage, not our money, and not our taxes.

Carey asked some questions about our income and expenses. In addition to the mortgage, utilities, and our daughter Andrea's college tuition, we were still paying medical expenses from Lou's double hip surgery three years earlier. Carey said the only solution on the taxes was an offer in compromise. In certain cases, he said, when taxpayers owe so much they cannot pay it back with their current income, the IRS will agree to reduce the amount owed. He drafted offers for us, which both the IRS and the Georgia Department of Revenue accepted. Then the first two checks I wrote every month were those tax checks.

Yet even after the compromise, there was not enough money left each month to pay the mortgage and other expenses. We were still sinking. So I contacted a well-known Christian financial consulting ministry and met with a counselor over several weeks. The man was so patient with me, but finally he said, "Mrs. Sulcer, I cannot advise you to declare bankruptcy. We have a policy against that. Yet I can't offer you any other solution. Your tax debt is so great, there is no possible way you can dig out of that and also address the medical expenses and the mortgage." Bankruptcy would not make the tax bill go away, and the mortgage company would take back my house.

At home, Kevin had quit the football team and was making choices out of anger and rebellion. He had been a black belt and national champion in karate at fourteen, with all the focus and self-discipline required for that level of success. Two years later his self-discipline had become self-doubt, and in his searching for answers, he was making terrible choices.

Lou was gone, Kevin was losing his way, and it seemed I could no longer build a family, despite my many years of teaching other women how to be godly wives and mothers. I was a complete, devastating failure in my most important responsibility, creating the model Christian home.

A Glimmer of Light

FIGHTING HARD against the darkness, I had asked my doctor to help, and she prescribed antidepressants. But after several months the pills weren't making much difference, and I wondered if I would ever be all right. Driving to a business meeting one morning, I suddenly heard someone in the car crying, and in an instant I realized it was me. I was sobbing. When I describe the event, it hardly seems possible, but I heard crying before I knew I was the one crying. It frightened me so much I pulled over to the side of the road to compose myself. What was going on? I had to get help. Somebody had to show me a way out.

Maybe our pastor, Clark Hutchinson, could help. I started the car and found a pay phone. Clark's secretary answered and could tell right away that I was in trouble. She told me to come to the back door of the church, and she would take me straight in.

I sat in Clark's office, bawling like a child. "I've lost all hope,"

I cried. "Hope was the only thing I had left, and now it's gone. It's like God has allowed a mockery to be made of my life and everything I stood for!"

Clark sat quietly for several seconds while I took a few deep breaths. "Now, Harriet," he said, "what you had is what you have, and that's Jesus. You cannot lose Him."

He was right. I had been putting my hope in hope instead of in Jesus. "But I've been praying and waiting, and nothing is happening," I said.

"Nothing you can see," Clark replied. "Something is happening. When God has begun a good work in you, He will see it through to completion. God is at work behind the scenes in ways that you and I are not aware."

I left the church that day feeling better, though my worst days were still ahead of me. Some days the darkness was so deep, I couldn't see even the faintest glimmer of light. I told myself to put my hope in Jesus. I read scripture and prayed so much, but the answers, the hope, wouldn't come. Lou was still gone, Kevin was still lost, and I was still frightened and confused.

In late spring, the Juice Plus Company scheduled a regional business meeting in Atlanta, and as a national marketing director, I was to be introduced to the five hundred attendees. Then I would host a luncheon at a Steak and Ale restaurant nearby for forty of my team members. It was a big responsibility and should have been an exciting time for me. But in the week leading up to the meeting I was feeling so fragile. If somebody had touched me, I might have fallen apart like an eggshell.

Our daughter Christy was on my Juice Plus team, and she came up from Sarasota, Florida, where her husband was playing minor league baseball for the Texas Rangers. Andrea was on her way home from her freshman year in college, and Kevin was spending the summer with friends from our church youth group who had moved to Canada. The night before the Juice Plus event,

I was feeling especially nervous and decided to double up on the antidepressants. It was important that I be at my best. If one pill wasn't working, maybe two would. But when I went to bed that night, my heart was racing, my stomach was queasy, and I had a headache. I tossed and turned all night, and finally, at five o'clock in the morning, I went to Christy's room and woke her up.

"I don't know what's happening," I said. "I haven't slept all night, and I'm so anxious. And I have this meeting today. I don't know what to do."

She reminded me that she would be at the meeting, and I began to relax. Looking back, I think I had subconsciously held on until Christy came home. She's so strong—such a take-charge person.

On the way out the door I picked up a Don Moen tape that had just come in the mail and put it in my purse. I subscribed to a tape-of-the-month of worship and praise music, and the new one had come that day. I thought we might listen to it in the car driving home.

I don't remember anything about the moments when I stood offstage and waited for my turn to step to the microphone. I was able to walk out and say, "Hi, I'm Harriet Sulcer, a national marketing director from Marietta" and walk off. And then an hour or so later, I welcomed my group for our luncheon. Nobody suspected that anything was wrong in my life.

Christy stood beside me while I was talking to other people, and after a while the room started spinning. I didn't know if I was going to faint or die, but something bad was happening. I turned to Christy and tried to whisper, "I think I'm going to faint."

"No," Christy said, "not here. Not now. I'm taking you to the restroom. You can faint when we get in there."

She put her arm in mine and pulled me tightly to her. Thankfully the restroom was close, and she guided me in before I passed out. Someone told the restaurant manager, who called

911 to make sure I was not having a heart attack. EMTs came and cleared me, and Christy and I went home. Christy tells the next part of the story:

> Mom was worn out, so I helped her get to bed. Then she was so confused, she couldn't put a sentence together. She needed to go to the hospital. When she sat on the side of the bed, and I tried to put her shoes on her, she asked me who I was and what I was trying to do. It didn't freak me out. That was the most amazing thing to me—that I had strength to work through the situation without being afraid. I knew that strength was not coming from me. It was strength from the Lord. I was able to talk to Mom in a real strong "mama" voice, and she followed my instructions.

Lying in that hospital bed, I knew—during those moments when I was able to "know"—that something was terribly wrong. A few times my thoughts were clear enough to suspect I was having a nervous breakdown, and my first concerns were for the people that I must be disappointing.

Did Mother and Daddy know? I had spent most of my married life trying to make peace between Mother and Daddy and Lou, not wanting to disappoint any of them and wanting so desperately for them to love each other. If Daddy knew about the breakdown, he would blame Lou. "It's all Lou's fault," he would say. "That's what put her there." One more brick in the wall of contempt they were building against him.

I didn't want the girls to call my brother, Richard, either. He would tell me, "You need to leave this man and forget that ever happened."

Kevin didn't know. He was in Canada. That was good.

Then I drifted away again. My memories of that hospital stay still come in pieces, and not in the right order. At some point the doctor came into the room, and I asked, "I'm having a nervous breakdown, aren't I?"

"Mrs. Sulcer," he said, "you're experiencing emotional exhaustion, and what you experienced today was a severe panic attack. Emotional overload, or perhaps an anxiety attack. We have to get to the root cause of this, or you will be back in here."

Richard came in from Kentucky. He spoke to the doctor right outside my room, and I heard the doctor tell him I was having a nervous breakdown. He used those words. Then Lou came in. I hadn't seen him in so long. He and Richard talked softly out in the hall.

On my second day in the hospital, Christy was looking for something in my purse and saw the Don Moen tape I had picked up. She thought listening to it might help me, so she asked Andrea to bring a portable tape player to the hospital. For the next two days I listened to that music over and over. One song engraved itself in my mind and on my heart: "Give thanks with a grateful heart."

The piano played so gently, like a quiet conversation, and Don Moen's voice was a friend offering his hand and saying, "Come with me. Here is a safe place."

He sang, "And now let the weak say, 'I am strong.' Let the poor say, 'I am rich, because of what the Lord has done for us.'"

For the first time in months I felt at peace. The one thing I knew was that God was with me in this place and speaking to me through Don Moen's voice. I was weak, but God could make me strong again. His presence was new and almost tangible. Finally somebody else was in charge.

Then Christy told me they were taking me home.

Into Your Hand

DESPITE THE words to the music I continued to play when we came home, and despite what the Lord had already done for me, I was not strong. But my daughters were.

If the phone rang, I trembled. I didn't know what to say to people who called, or even to the girls. All my thoughts were confused. After a day or two, Christy and Andrea established some ground rules. First, no telephone. "We've seen how the telephone upsets you," Christy said. "For now, you don't need to talk to anybody. Andrea is going to answer the phone and screen your calls, and she's telling everybody right now that you need time. You'll return their calls when you can."

Fortunately the team I had built in my business was self-sufficient. When they called, Andrea told them I was taking a six-week sabbatical.

Second, no visitors. I was not ready to see even my closest friends.

The third rule was my own: no more antidepressants. Christy was right. My depression was not clinical; it was spiritual. In over a year, the tranquilizers had not worked. Andrea threw away the bottle.

Only God could heal me now. My only hope was to put myself completely in His hands.

"Into your hand I commit my spirit."

Those were Jesus' last words on the cross. He was speaking Psalm 31:5, which David, the psalmist, had written when he was suffering deep depression and discouragement. David's song finished with remarkable praise and trust in God:

You saw my affliction
and knew the anguish of my soul. . . .
My life is consumed by anguish, . . .
my strength fails. . . .
But I trust in you, LORD;
I say, "You are my God."
My times are in your hands.
—vv. 7, 10, 14–15

David's hope was my hope and my family's hope.
Only God.

My Daughters' Strength

I COULDN'T sleep by myself at night. When I lay in bed I felt
anxious and absolutely alone. Andrea got me into my pajamas,
put me to bed, and then came to bed and slept beside me. She
was nineteen and had just finished her freshman year at the University of Alabama and was working that summer as a pool manager. As strong as Christy was, Andrea was quiet and steady, just
what I needed through the summer after Christy went back home
to Florida.

In the morning, Andrea packed a little lunch and took me to
work with her. She led me to a chair on the pool deck, started the
tape player, and put the earphones in my ear while more worship
music played. An hour later she came over and changed the tape
to an audio version of the Bible. That's all I did. No reading. No
talking. Just sitting and listening. The next day we did the same
thing. After work she bought groceries, cooked supper and made
sure I ate, then paid bills and took care of the house.

Christy and Andrea were strong enough to carry me because
Lou had made them strong. We had lived on a farm for five years
when our children were young, and they all had chores. At the

end of the day or on weekends, Lou taught them to fish. He also taught them to clean what they caught. I stood at the window and watched Andrea, when she was six years old, scaling fish, gutting them with a sharp knife, and dropping the heads and guts into a bucket beside the table. That's the way Lou's mother had taught him, and he was going to make sure his daughters knew how. He wanted them strong, like his mother.

Christy came running into the house one day. Lou had caught a huge snake out in the chicken house and dispatched it. Christy wasn't a bit scared or grossed out. She was awed—impressed that her daddy could do anything to keep that chicken farm going. Nothing ever fazed or stumped him. If a chicken was sick or injured, he wrung its neck and tossed it into the pit out back. If a machine was broken, he fixed it.

Every morning Lou ran several miles to relieve stress; that was his outlet. Christy started waking up and running with him, just to be with her father. She told me one day she wished she could be a boy so she could be like her daddy. All their life Lou told his children how proud he was because they were growing up tough.

I now needed tough and strong. Christy delivered at the hospital. Andrea was strong for me at home. In her first summer from college, when her friends were getting together and having fun, I could not function. She became my strength, beside me every moment of every day, holding me up.

Be Still and Know

WHEN I WAS a teenager, I woke up early every morning and had breakfast in the kitchen with Daddy. Mornings in the Mississippi Delta were so still. Daddy taught me how to make coffee in the percolator and build the fire. Some of my most precious memories are the smell of fresh coffee and fireplace smoke with my father on a quiet, cold, winter morning long before the sun rose.

Later in the day Mother filled the house with the sweet aromas of homemade pastries she made in case friends dropped by. If she was caught unprepared by an unexpected guest, she might quickly bake some little pumpkin breads, a specialty of hers, in tin cans. Cinnamon, nutmeg, ginger, orange zest all baking together. When she took the bread out of the oven, she sliced it and served it with cream cheese—and coffee. Always coffee.

Two of the things I missed most during my summer of rest were friends and coffee. When I stopped taking the antidepressants, I couldn't touch caffeine. A single cup of coffee left me shaky and nervous. And I wasn't strong enough to visit even with my closest friends. I couldn't collect my thoughts and felt unsure and nervous about everything. Martie, Sheila, Jackie, and I had been praying together for nearly thirty years. I knew they were praying for me now, but I wasn't ready to see them.

Day by day I grew stronger sitting in the sunshine by the pool, listening to my music and the Bible. The warmth felt like God's embrace as He spoke softly to me. Later I listened to R. C. Sproul's series on The Holiness of God, searching for truth. I was starting to pursue God. Sometimes I became anxious, and He told me to slow down, or even stop. He would come to me.

"Be still, and know that I am God."

Time after time He spoke these words of Psalm 46:10 into my heart. He was in control. I might go to a scary place in my mind, thinking about Kevin or my financial ruin. Fear and sorrow would start rising up around me like a flood, and I would try to run to God. He would say, "Be still. I am God. Your life may feel out of control, but I am not out of control. Your life is in the palm of My hand."

Then one day it occurred to me that if my life was in His

palm, He must have opened His hand to allow in all the things that were happening to me. And if He let these things in, I didn't have to run from them or fear them.

After supper I told Andrea, "I think I can make it. I would like to sleep in my own bed tonight."

"Are you sure?" she asked.

"I think so."

I GREW stronger, and after six weeks of quiet, it was time to re-connect with the world and go back to work. Richard called from Kentucky and asked Kevin and me to move up there. He and his wife, Dianne, had room in their home for us, and we could make a fresh start. My parents also said I could move back home to Mississippi. But leaving Georgia would mean giving up hope of reconciling with Lou, and I wasn't ready for that. Also, we couldn't uproot Kevin just as his senior year was beginning. We would stay and face whatever difficulties lay ahead.

I called Lou and we scheduled a meeting with a lawyer to discuss the foreclosure proceedings on the house and the process of declaring bankruptcy. The lawyer explained that bankruptcy would allow most of our debts to be forgiven, but it would remain on our records for seven years. During that time it would be almost impossible to obtain new credit. He also said he saw no other choice for us. What the lawyer didn't tell us was that losing our home to foreclosure would be like a death in the family and another step in the disintegration of our family.

We left the office and started looking for a place for Kevin and me to live.

Financial Rock Bottom

FOR THE next year, Kevin and I lived in a rental house. I continued to build my business while God rebuilt me, and Kevin struggled through his senior year in high school. Lou never filed for divorce, and his indecision left us paralyzed. He dropped by the house unannounced several times, saying he just wanted to check on us.

"Please, Lou," I told him, "either come home or file for divorce. Kevin needs his father, and we both need to know what to expect. You've left us sitting like patients in the waiting room. That's the hardest part of going to the doctor—waiting without knowing. We need a resolution."

But Lou did not commit either way. In the meantime, I continued to make payments to the IRS and the Georgia Department of Revenue. Kevin graduated and started college, and not long after he left, my banker called and insisted I come in right away. I hurried to the bank, and she told me the Georgia Department of Revenue had seized my account. "They've taken everything you have," she said.

"How can they do that?" I asked. "They accepted our offer in compromise, and I haven't missed a single payment. I'm early every month."

"Someone at DOR changed his mind," she said. "Your balance is zero."

"But I just mailed checks to pay all my bills yesterday," I said. "Are they all going to bounce?"

"They are," she said. "We'll have to return all of them as 'insufficient funds.' You need to call those people right away, and believe me, if you tell them the Georgia Department of Revenue is coming after you, they'll be sympathetic."

"Can't I just put money back in the account?"

"DOR put a lien on the account," she said. "Anything you put in, they'll take right out until the debt is satisfied."

I was starting to panic. Where would I keep money? How would I pay bills?

"So what do I do?" I asked.

"You'll have to pay everything with cash and money orders," she said.

I tried to picture that. People stand in line at the post office for money orders, and I wondered why they did that or how it worked. Apparently I was about to learn.

I left the bank, drove straight home, went to bed—I didn't know what else to do—and lay there for hours. Over and over my mind raced through the possibilities, all of them bad. I could call the phone company and Georgia Power and tell them my problem, but I didn't have cash to pay the bills when the checks bounced. My next paycheck was two weeks away. They would cut off the phone and the electricity. Then the rent check would bounce.

I didn't know what to do or who to call. My parents would be devastated. I had rejected my brother's advice, so I couldn't call him. We hadn't spoken in weeks. We weren't estranged—just strained. For hours I lay on the bed, tossing and turning through the night. When dawn broke, there was no revelation, no peace, no hope.

The phone rang early in the morning, and I let it go for several rings. How could it be anything but trouble? Finally I willed myself out of bed and answered, "Hello."

"Harriet?"

It was Richard. Oh, what a blessing to hear my brother's voice.

"Sorry to call so early," he said. "I just had you on my mind this morning. We haven't talked in a while, and I'll be isolated for the next two weeks in flight training."

He paused, waiting for me to respond, but I didn't say anything—couldn't say anything. I knew if I tried to talk, the tears would come pouring out.

"Harriet, are you okay?" he asked. "You sound—"

I was crying before he finished his sentence. Crying hard.

"Harriet?"

I took a few deep breaths before I was able to respond, "No, I'm not okay."

"What's wrong?"

Again I composed myself enough to explain what had happened—the meeting at the bank. "I have nothing," I said. "Zero balance, and what's worse, I mailed out checks to pay bills yesterday."

"Okay," Richard said after listening to everything, and I could feel him taking control. "Let's work through this. The first thing you need to do is get yourself a shower and get some breakfast. Then get all your bills together and call me back and let me know the total. We're going to work this out, okay?"

"Okay," I said. "Thank you, Richard."

I hung up the phone and started crying again, but this time the tears were relief. I was no longer alone. I showered and ate breakfast, like Richard suggested, then added up the numbers. Seeing the total gave me confidence. Richard could help me figure out a way.

When I called him back, he had a plan. "I'll call Carey Barnes and wire the money to him," he said. "That will keep it out of your account, and Carey can give you the cash you need to pay your bills. I'll be out for a couple of weeks, so I'm sending enough to get you through until I get back."

I sat down and began to wonder again what would have happened if Richard hadn't called. God had nudged his heart, and he had responded.

When I told Carey about the call from my banker, he said he had never heard of DOR seizing assets in a situation like mine, where the taxpayer was making payments as agreed. "But if they did this once," he said, "you need to have a plan to take care of the debt even more aggressively than your agreement with them."

"How can I pay them any faster?" I asked. "They're already getting everything but my rent and food money."

"You need to get out of the rental house," he told me. "You need to use every penny you make to pay off the tax debt."

"How?" I asked. "Where will I go?"

Carey paused, and then he made the most generous offer I could imagine.

"Sheila and I have a room in our basement," he said. "It isn't very big, but it won't cost you anything."

"Carey, I can't do that. That's a huge burden on the two of you."

"Of course it's not a burden. Sheila and I want to do this."

Sheila and Carey had been two of our closest friends for years, and their son Barron and Kevin were best friends. But their generosity was beyond anything I could have imagined.

No Mercy

SURELY I could reason with the man at the Georgia Department of Revenue. After all, the IRS had not come down on me like this. I had not missed a payment to either the IRS or the Georgia DOR. If I was honest about our circumstances and humbled myself before him, he would be reasonable.

I carefully wrote out what I would say to him and read it over and over, editing it and trying to get it just right. "I understand we are in a situation that we created, but please understand that I am a single mother right now. My husband is not living at home. I'm trying the best I can. We have been negligent. We have not fulfilled our responsibility, but I'm trying to be rehabilitated as a taxpayer and make this right. We have an offer in compromise, and I have not been late with a single payment."

I went in at the appointed time and sat with a dozen other

people in a waiting room. They called me in, and I explained my situation. I might as well have been talking to the wall instead of the man behind the desk.

"Mrs. Sulcer," he said, "I'm sorry you got yourself into this mess, but you're going to have to get yourself out of it."

"If I could only help you understand the situation you've put me in," I said. "I have a home-based business. I can't pay you what I owe you unless I can continue to operate my business. Now you've put me in a position where I can't even put gas in my car. How can I pay you back? How can I be rehabilitated? You've tied my hands behind me, and I don't have any resources."

"You people think you can go out there and make all this money and not pay your taxes," he said.

"Sir, I've told you that we did not handle it properly, and I want to do the right thing. Please give me a chance to do it right."

"I'm sorry," he said, and then he just sat there.

"Would you leave a hundred dollars in my personal account so I can buy groceries?"

"No, ma'am, I will not."

And those were his last words to me: "No, ma'am, I will not."

I started crying like a child. I don't know if he stood up or if I just walked out. But I went through the room with all those people waiting to see him, and I was sobbing. I'm sure I didn't raise their hopes. I cried all the way down the elevator and out to my car, then I opened the door and threw myself across the front seat.

"God!" I cried. "How is this going to work? How?"

LORD MY SHEPHERD
Jehovah-raah

*The Lord was caring tenderly for Lou and me long
before we knew each other. He brought us together in
a covenant relationship, and protected us as our
family grew and then fell apart.*

1940–1991

Strike Your Match!

AS A BOY in the 1940s, Louie Sulcer had dreamed of playing professional baseball. For the first nine years of his life, his family lived in five different houses in midtown Atlanta, all of them within walking distance of Ponce de Leon Park, where the Atlanta Crackers minor league baseball team played. Louie loved the Crackers. On summer nights he could see the glow of the ballpark and picture himself playing second base. Whenever he had fifty cents, and the Crackers were playing an afternoon game, he walked over to watch. He took his glove in case a fly ball came his way.

In 1950, shortly after the season ended, Rev. Billy Graham brought a six-week crusade to Ponce de Leon Park. A stage was built in center field facing the infield and the stands, and Louie walked over to the ballpark to see what it was all about. Billy Graham was young and energetic, and on the first night of the crusade more than twenty-five thousand people attended.

Louie walked right out onto the infield through the crowd of adults to get a closer look at the young evangelist with his white suit and red Bible. Louie didn't have his baseball glove, of course, but standing on the grass and looking around at all the people in the bleachers under the lights, he must have imagined himself playing second base. He listened to the preaching, and at the end of the service Billy Graham asked everyone to close their eyes. "The conversion of one person is like striking a match in the Hollywood Bowl," Rev. Graham told the crowd. "Won't you strike your match for God?"

Then he called on those who wanted to "find the way to

Jesus Christ" to raise their hands. While the organ played softly, eleven-year-old Louie raised his hand. He was ready to strike a match. Rev. Graham directed him and others to a tent in right field, where volunteers served as counselors for those professing their faith. Louie went back to see Billy Graham several more times over the weeks, and one night he convinced his parents to go with him to the ballpark, where they, too, gave their lives to Christ. He would talk about that crusade and its impact for the rest of his life.

Father and Son

IN 1948 Louie Sulcer Sr. opened a restaurant on Forsyth Street in downtown Atlanta, right across from the main Atlanta post office and a block south of Rich's, Atlanta's premier department store. He called it the Postal Café, and it was open from breakfast through supper. Every table and every seat at the counter was filled with postal workers right before and after a shift change. Mr. Sulcer bussed the counter and helped at the grill, but mainly he greeted every customer who came in the door. He was a thin man who ran on coffee and cigarettes, and in the restaurant he was always moving.

He woke up at four o'clock every morning to get downtown and open up, and he didn't come home until sometime after nine o'clock every night, six days a week. He ate thousands of meals with thousands of strangers but almost never with his family. He slept all day Sunday just to catch up so he could start over on Monday morning. Mr. Sulcer's children, Louie Jr. and Linda, never remembered being hugged by their father or told, "I love you."

But he must have loved them, because when his son was a teenager, he didn't want him working at the café. He didn't want young Louie to follow in his footsteps in the diner business. Louie Sulcer Sr. had come to Atlanta alone when he was sixteen years old in the early 1920s, looking for work. Life didn't have to be that hard for his children.

Lou could grow up playing games, especially baseball and football. His parents bought a small home on Park Circle in Buckhead, on the north side of town, and he enjoyed a typical childhood—wearing braces, taking trumpet lessons, and playing with lots of friends. When he was young and the Postal Café was thriving, his mother drove a Cadillac and wore a fur coat, and by the time he entered North Fulton High School, he was strong and fast, though small—just right for playing second base and running back. In 1955, his junior year, the football team finished 9–1. Halfback "Little Louie Sulcer," as he was known in the *Atlanta Journal*, ran with "a stable of runaway thoroughbreds."

His parents never attended his games. His father could not leave the restaurant, and his mother was absolutely terrified of seeing her son injured on the field. But every Friday night during the season, she would sit close by the radio and listen to the games. "If they said Louie was down on the field," Lou's sister, Linda, remembers, "she would turn it off and walk away, then come back later and turn it back on." When Mr. Sulcer came home from the café, she would tell him all about the game. On Saturday morning she would cut the article about the game from the newspaper and tape it in a scrapbook. Lou was still turning the pages of that scrapbook fifty years later.

Injuries slowed "Little Louie Sulcer" in his senior year—he was cleated in the thigh and had surgery to remove a calcium deposit—but he was still able to play in the Georgia All-Star game and get a shot at his dream, playing football at Georgia Tech. By that time, however, life had grown harder for the Sulcer family. The café was struggling. Lou worked around the corner from home at the construction site of Lenox Square the summer before his freshman year at Tech to help his family with finances. Football didn't go so well his freshman year, with more injuries and another surgery.

The Postal Café went out of business. Relatives brought food and money to help the family while Mr. Sulcer searched for a job, and after a while, he went to work at the Tastee Freez on Northside Drive. Nine-year-old Linda felt sorry for her father, who was making a living scooping ice cream cones for kids. He kept looking for something better, and finally became restaurant manager at Seven Steers steakhouse, but he was spiraling. When the breakdown came, he was admitted to the hospital for treatments. After he was released, he continued to receive the treatments, which lifted him temporarily each time. Lou saw his father's depression, his downward slide, his multiple hospital stays, and the treatments that continued for years, and often wondered if that would be his own future.

Lou couldn't stay in school when the restaurant closed. He needed to help his family, so he left Tech after his freshman year and enlisted in the navy before he would have been drafted, and was assigned to the Atlanta Naval Air Station. When he completed active duty, he went to work in the real estate department at C&S Bank and remained a member of the navy reserves.

My Father's Dreams for Me

MY PARENTS had dreams for me.

While Louie Sulcer Jr. was growing up in Atlanta, I was living in Hollandale, in the Mississippi Delta. Every family in the Delta had a history tied to the land, and every child was known first by, "Who's your mama and daddy?" If you were a Stovall in the Delta, that meant something.

My father's father, Peter Simpson Stovall, was a large landowner in the Delta and was treasurer of the State of Mississippi from 1912 to 1916. He even ran for governor in 1915 but lost. He and his wife, Anna, lived in Greenville, on the banks of the Mississippi River. They had eighteen children, six girls and twelve boys, including my father, who was one of the youngest of the eighteen.

In 1922, when Daddy was thirteen, his father died. The older sons helped their mother with the farm, but in 1927 the worst flood in the history of the United States swept across the Mississippi Valley. The river broke through a levy near Greenville and ten days later covered a million acres of the Delta with ten feet of water. It would be months before the waters receded. Daddy started college at Ole Miss, then the Depression hit, and their money, which was tied to the land, pretty much ran out by Daddy's sophomore year. That ended his formal education.

The money was gone but opportunities were not. As a young man, Daddy built a cottonseed export business to South and Central America, and he became quite successful, though he never graduated from college.

My mother did not grow up in the Delta in a white-glove society, but in Bon Homme, a community just south of Hattiesburg, on the other side of the state. Her father worked for the railroad and played the violin. Her grandfather was a country doctor. Mother could be comfortable at the country club, leading the garden club, or sitting around a campfire. In fact, she preferred the campfire. When she smelled wood smoke, she told Daddy it was time to get the tent out.

I was their only daughter, and Daddy treated me like a princess. He expected other people to treat me the same way, and he believed I would marry a wealthy young man from the Delta who would shower me with his affection the way he always had.

In the early 1950s, when I became a teenager, I knew exactly what I wanted to do with my life. I would become a wife and a mother in a Christian home like the one where I had grown up. My goal was lined up with my parents' dreams. Those were the expectations of young girls all over the United States in our generation. Mother and Daddy sent me to charm school (all the Delta girls went), which reinforced many of the lessons my mother had already taught me about being a young lady: how to greet people, how to get in and out of a car politely, how to be seated gracefully.

One huge expectation for Delta girls was that we make our debut into society, with five weeks of parties leading up to the Delta Debutante Ball in December. That was our "coming out." After my sophomore year in college I was invited to become a Delta Debutante, and I told Mother and Daddy I didn't want to do it. I wasn't the debutante type. Parties and gowns and all that pomp were for other girls, not me. But in my heart I knew I couldn't disappoint my parents. The Delta was their home, and the Debutante Ball was an important part of their life in the Delta. I had two first cousins coming out that season. How could I not want to be with all the other Stovall girls? Then one night when my father was out of the room, my mother confided, "This means so much to your daddy." She had no idea of the power of those words. I said okay.

I hardly knew my escort for the ball, who was the son of a Delta landowner.

Looking back, I don't think my parents could see that the world they wanted me to live in was dying. Daddy was a dreamer.

Part of the Family

IF YOU'VE read *The Help* or seen the movie, then you know a little about the world I grew up in. The story was set in Jackson but filmed in Greenwood, in the Delta. Hollandale was in the heart of the Delta, cotton country.

Whenever anybody talks about Mississippi in the 1950s and '60s, race invariably becomes part of the conversation. My children remember Irma Jean, who worked alongside my mother in our home, and Hubbard Hundley, who was foreman at my father's plant, as "part of the family." That's a phrase that white people in the South used for decades to describe their black servants. I don't know if the black servants would have considered themselves part of the white families. I can only tell you about my family.

One night when I was growing up in the mid-1950s, we went to dinner at the VFW Café, the only place to eat out in Hollandale. We were waiting for our food when someone came over to our table and whispered something to my mother. Her expression went dark, and when the man left, she told my father, "Peter, we have to go."

"What?" Daddy asked. "Why?

"They've arrested a boy and put him in jail." (She said the boy's family name. He was African American, and Mother and Daddy knew his parents.)

"Well, what are you going to do about it?" Daddy asked.

"We're going to get him out," Mother said. "He's thirteen years old. He's not safe in the jail."

So we all got up and left.

I don't know why the boy had been arrested, but we walked from the café to the jail, and my parents did whatever it took to get him out—whether it was to pay his bail or just talk to the sheriff.

My mother knew how to walk a fine line in a world where a black person could not enter the front door of the VFW Café. She made no secret of her commitment to her neighbors across the tracks, but she didn't make a show of it either.

She became close friends with Professor Sanders, who was principal at the African American school in town. (I think people called him "Professor" because they had a hard time calling him "Mister.") Mother believed the best way to narrow the gap between black and white was to influence the next generation. She asked Professor Sanders to keep an eye out for sharp young men that he thought had a chance if they could get them out of the

Delta during their teenage years. Mother would take those young men on as a cause.

She connected with Piney Woods School, near Jackson, which had a great reputation for preparing African American students for college. I'm not sure how she did it, but somehow she raised scholarship money for students from Hollandale. There must have been other people in town who agreed with her and were willing to help. More than once Mother told Daddy at Sunday dinner, "Peter, we need to go over to Piney Woods next week. We have a young man ready to go."

Her reputation led to invitations to speak at the black Baptist church in Hollandale.

Daddy was president of a cottonseed delinting company that employed a lot of African American workers, including Hubbard, the same man my children saw working at my parents' house years later. Hubbard was a big man—he always seemed like a giant to me.

From five-thirty until six o'clock every morning, Daddy and Hubbard sat together in Daddy's office having coffee and planning the day. Daddy relied on Hubbard to keep the plant running smoothly, especially when Daddy was on a sales trip to South America. Spending so much time together every day, they talked about family and children and dreams for their children. Hubbard wasn't just "a member of the family." He truly became Daddy's best friend. I believe either of them would have given his life for the other.

Our family spent a lot of time on the water, and Daddy decided it would be fun for us to have a pontoon boat out on Lake Washington. He told Hubbard about his plan one morning, and the two of them decided they could build it together.

They were pretty far along with construction and had put the boat in the water while they built the extras that made it special. They used a barrel to make a grill with a top so we could have picnics out on the lake.

They were out there one Saturday afternoon, and Daddy asked Hubbard to do something that required him to lean over the back of the boat. Hubbard leaned out, lost his grip, and tumbled over into the water.

Daddy didn't take three seconds to evaluate the situation. Hubbard couldn't swim, and he was much bigger and stronger than Daddy. And a desperate, drowning man can take his rescuer to the bottom with him. But there was no way Daddy was going to watch his best friend go under. He jumped in and was able to get Hubbard back into the boat.

Word spread fast in the black community that Daddy had saved Hubbard's life, and for weeks I saw people come up to him on the street and thank him. It made me proud to be his daughter.

Years later Hubbard's wife called my parents. Hubbard had passed away in the night. "His last desire," she told Daddy, "was that Miss Harriet would preach his funeral."

Mother said it was her finest honor. She stood in the pulpit and spoke of the love and respect Daddy and Hubbard had for each other. "So in Christ Jesus you are all children of God through faith, for all of you who were baptized into Christ have clothed yourselves with Christ. There is neither Jew nor Gentile, neither slave nor free, nor is there male and female, for you are all one in Christ Jesus. If you belong to Christ, then you are Abraham's seed, and heirs according to the promise" (Galatians 3:26–29).

Hope and a Future

THE ATLANTA school system sent recruiters to colleges all over the South looking for teachers. The thought of moving to Atlanta had never crossed our minds, but when Tricia, an attractive young recruiter, came to Ole Miss and told us all about their schools and how much she loved living in Atlanta, three of my sorority sisters and I decided to go. What an adventure for girls from Mississippi to go to Atlanta. It was like going to New York City.

I had majored in home economics, and I had more in common with the Delta Debs than I cared to admit. I didn't want a career. I wanted to be a wife and mother. In the place and time where I grew up, most of the women became homemakers. That was the plan. Husbands took care of finances, and wives ran the home and did social and philanthropic work. The woman's work was not inconsequential. My mother never "worked" a day in her life, but she worked all the time, volunteering in our community and church and running our home like a machine. She often entertained friends and Daddy's business associates. And she maintained a big, beautiful garden.

I moved to Atlanta when I graduated from Ole Miss in 1963 and started teaching at Birney Elementary School. Anybody who was young and single in Atlanta in the 1960s will tell you the city was an exciting place to live—and you'll hear many different definitions of "exciting." I shared an apartment on Biscayne Drive in Buckhead with three roommates, and we enjoyed the big-city social scene. I had completely avoided alcohol at Ole Miss and even the champagne at debutante parties, but now I asked myself, why not? Everybody else was doing it. I didn't get carried away with the party crowd, but I enjoyed dating and becoming part of the scene.

All the way from Mississippi, my best friend, Rusty Armstrong, and my brother, who had just started college, sensed the change. Rusty and I had grown up like sisters, and when she graduated from college she joined the staff of Campus Crusade for Christ. She and Richard drove over and lovingly confronted me: "Where are you going with all this?"

Their concern touched my heart and was a wake-up call. I hadn't become a prodigal by any stretch. I had grown up in the church. My family had always been active in the church. I hadn't started going to church in Atlanta yet, but I would at some point. I was living a pretty normal life for a young adult woman in the city in the mid-1960s.

Rusty invited me to a Campus Crusade meeting at Georgia Tech. Tech was experiencing a revival of sorts at the time, led mostly by football players and Tech campus director Jon Braun. Several players and other students stood up and passionately shared their testimony like nothing I had ever seen. Sitting on the front row, I could see their sincerity and feel their emotion, and I was drawn to these people. I'd been to the Baptist Student Union at Ole Miss, but I hadn't seen passion like this. It was like experiencing the living Christ for the first time. I wanted what they had! Then Jon spoke, and though I don't remember much of his talk, I'll never forget when he said, "There is a God-sized vacuum inside every soul that only God can fill." He was talking about me.

We sang a song at the end of the night, and I know Jon saw the hunger in my eyes, because as soon as the music ended, he walked straight toward me, like he knew what I was thinking.

We had met earlier in the evening, so he called me by name. "Harriet," he asked, "do you know Jesus in a personal, intimate way?"

I couldn't collect the words to answer him. I knew Jesus. I had known Him since I was eight years old and walked down the aisle of our little church in Hollandale, Mississippi, given my life to Him, and been baptized. Now I was sitting in a Campus Crusade for Christ meeting surrounded by other young people. Anybody looking at my life at that point would have said I had everything going for me at twenty-one. But there was a gnawing emptiness inside me that I could not explain, and Jon knew it. I thought the thing I was missing was a person to share my life with, but Jon knew that wasn't the answer.

I broke. The tears I had held back suddenly flowed, and it was a minute or more before I could finally say, "No, I don't."

"But you want to, don't you?" Jon asked me.

"Yes, I do."

"It's really very simple, Harriet. You just have to open your heart totally and fully to the Lord Jesus Christ and let Him be the love of your life."

That's what I did that night. I took one step toward opening my heart to Christ, and life was never the same again. I began to fall in love with Him. At twenty-one, I got it—like a light turning on. Now when I share my faith, that's the point I go back to.

My Father had dreams for me. "'For I know the plans I have for you,' declares the LORD, 'plans to prosper you and not to harm you, plans to give you hope and a future'" (Jeremiah 29:11).

Love, Death, and a Challenge

ON A GLORIOUS Saturday afternoon in November 1963, a friend who had graduated from Florida State took me on a date to the Georgia Tech–FSU football game. At a party after the game we were introduced to the couple across the table from us, Louie Sulcer and his date. It turned out that Lou's date was also "just a friend," and a few days later he called and asked me out.

Much of our conversation that evening centered on Lou's family. His father was at the point of death with cancer. His sister, Linda, was sixteen, his mother had never worked outside the home, and he was worried about them. Lou worked in the real estate department of C&S Bank, and I wondered how he might be helping his mother out.

He asked me out again, and our dates were low-key. We might go to a movie or to Henri's, a wonderful little bakery and café. Lou wanted me to meet his family, but with Mr. Sulcer so sick, it didn't seem like the right time.

Lou's father died later in November. I met Mrs. Sulcer and Linda for the first time just a few days after the funeral when Lou took me by their house. He seemed so sensitive to his mother's needs.

Even in the sadness, we were falling in love. Lou was strong and kind and thoughtful.

In January he asked me to marry him. I said yes, and we set the date for Easter weekend, March 28, when I would have a break from school. Then we went to Mississippi to talk with my parents.

One of Daddy's first questions for Lou was, "Are you going back to school, son?"

"Yes sir," Lou said, although we hadn't discussed that possibility.

Daddy was looking out for his daughter and (he hoped) his future grandchildren. He was a successful businessman and loved to make friends. At restaurants he called the waiter by name, and by the time dinner was over he would have met the people at every adjacent table. When he talked to people, he listened and remembered. The second time he saw you, he would call your name and ask something specific about your family.

Those gifts became his most important assets when he was growing an export business, traveling all over Latin America selling cottonseed and barely able to speak a word of Spanish. He called his high school Spanish teacher, who lived in Leland, and she translated his correspondence so he could stay in touch with his friends and customers. (If she was disappointed that Daddy didn't remember any of his Spanish, she didn't show it.)

He also knew the importance of a college education, even though he had built his business without one. Lou saw something in Daddy's countenance as they talked, because in time he accepted the question about his education as a positive challenge.

"Trust Me"

LAKES DON'T freeze in the Mississippi Delta, so I didn't know anything about ice-skating.

"Take my hand," Lou said.

I was scared to death. We had gone to Highlands, North Carolina, for the weekend with three other couples, and they were skating on a frozen lake. There was no way it could be safe.

"I've done this so many times," Lou said. "Trust me."

Finally I reached out and let him take my hand to pull me slowly out onto the lake. My feet didn't move. I just glided as he pulled, and then I was skating slowly alongside him, on solid ice, never letting go of his hand.

The moment was magical, one of the most romantic times of my life, as we skated around that lake surrounded by the snow-covered shoreline in the middle of the forest.

Marriage requires so much trust—in your spouse and in God. Lou and I were married just a few weeks after that winter trip, and I was just beginning to understand that concept.

Passages

MY MOTHER turned our Baptist church in Hollandale into a little Eden for our wedding, with a profusion of flowers, candles, and lights. She could do magic with flower arrangements, and she worked with the florist to go all out on the Saturday before Easter 1964.

Daddy walked me down the same aisle I had walked as an eight-year-old to proclaim Christ, and past the same pew where I had fallen asleep so many times with my head in his lap. The piano playing "Wedding March" was the same one I had played for church services as a high school senior.

My family was everywhere. That's the way it is when you have forty-one first cousins. Linda Fay, my cousin and college roommate, had offered her wedding gown, which her mother, Aunt Thelma, had sewn. She and another cousin, Dot, were two of my bridesmaids. I was so much a part of this place in the Delta.

And there stood my bridegroom, the handsome city boy who was taking me away, surrounded by his friends, who stood as groomsmen, and his sister, who was one of my bridesmaids. Lou's mother stood alone at her pew, a widow for only four months.

We would be going back to Atlanta, leaving my world along Deer Creek to live in theirs. So many of my friends and cousins had married Delta boys and never left home. I had been gone for two years, but this walk on my father's arm to Lou's would confirm my passage.

Back in Atlanta, Lou and I rented an apartment in Roswell Court, across the street from Peachtree Presbyterian Church. It was so popular, we had stayed on the waiting list until somebody moved out. Roswell Court was a beautiful place with a huge courtyard—a wide lawn, green grass, and lots of old shade trees. We could walk to Henri's and an ice cream shop nearby or knock on friends' doors and find a group getting together.

Lou followed up on his commitment to Daddy, enrolling at Georgia State University at night and majoring in finance. It may have been the right choice financially, but we should have been connecting as a couple in those early years. So many nights Lou went from work to school and then came home late, and I was alone in the apartment.

One weekend I was talking on the phone with my parents, and I told them I missed my piano. I had played since I was a little girl, and as a teenager I even played on Sundays at church. The next week, Daddy rented a U-Haul and brought my piano and the Baptist hymnal. Lou and some friends got it into our apartment, and we had it tuned. That night I opened the hymnal and started playing. Whenever Lou was at school, the piano and the hymns became my companion, and I never felt like I was alone.

The Crusade House

Jon and Mary Ellen Braun lived with their young children in a two-story, brick, colonial-style home at the corner of West Wesley Road and Peachtree Road. The house had been donated to Campus Crusade for Christ, and everybody called it the Crusade House. That house became a hangout for a lot of young people in Atlanta; Campus Crusade was not just for college students.

Mary Ellen encouraged us to share our faith with others—something I had never felt comfortable doing. Jon said that through Crusade he had learned to sit down to talk with a college student and guide the conversation to God in about fifteen seconds—to gauge if the student was interested. Mary Ellen suggested we invite friends into our homes, where we could discuss our faith in a more relaxed setting.

I followed my mother's model of hospitality and invited eight friends over for coffee and pastries I had made that morning. Several were the wives of Lou's high school friends, and three of them—Sheila Barnes, Marion Spence, and Martie Hunter—would begin a journey of faith and friendship with me that would last all our lives. Today we are sharing prayer requests for our grandchildren.

Lou and I Make a Promise

LOU STRUNG up a hammock between two trees alongside Dick's Creek, right where the cold water spilled over a huge boulder into a pool. It was late spring, about a month into trout season, and I still needed a sweater in the cool mountain air. I climbed into the hammock with my book and made myself comfortable, and Lou walked over to the creek with his rod and reel. He fished all day and I read all day, putting down my book to cheer him on when he called out to say he'd caught another one.

At the end of the day he built a campfire and told me how he had come to love these mountains.

During Easter break of his junior year in high school, he and thirteen friends all went camping together. They convinced their parents that they were old enough to go alone, and on Thursday afternoon they piled into three cars and drove north toward the Georgia mountains.

They drove to Lake Yonah, right below the Tugaloo power dam, and arrived early enough to canoe across to the South Carolina side before dark to set up camp. They camped there until Sunday morning, when Powell Hunter led them in an Easter service.

Charlie Breithaupt, Lou, Billy Jackson, and a few others went back to the mountains several times that summer and camped at Black Rock Mountain and Tallulah Gorge, or if they got a late start, they put up a tent beside the road. They all worked jobs in summer, so they couldn't take off until Friday afternoon. Most Fridays they were chasing the sun to get to a campsite by dark.

For years before we met, Lou would drive up to north Georgia himself on a Friday afternoon, pitch a tent near Jack's River or the Chestatee River or Dick's Creek and then wake up on Saturday and fish all day. The first time he invited me to join him, a few weeks after we married, I told him I didn't want to fish but would love to go camping with him. I had grown up in a family that enjoyed the outdoors, and we did a lot of tent camping. But when we drove up from Atlanta, the north Georgia mountains were totally different from the Mississippi Delta. The muddy water back home meandered slowly through the flatlands. Deer Creek flowed wide and slow and flat through my hometown, and spring rains drove it from its banks into the swamps. In north Georgia the cold, clear water crashed down steep mountainsides past laurels and rhododendrons blooming pink and white.

Night fell, and the forest went black except for the few stars that could squeeze a little light through the trees above us. The volume on the tumbling water seemed to turn up a notch, and the forest grew larger. Lou and I sat there without speaking, alone in God's incredible creation.

We sat a long time before Lou said, "Harriet, someday we're going to have a place up here."

It was like he had plucked the idea straight from my heart, and I hadn't even known it was there. What a thrilling idea— to build something together in this beautiful place. "Promise me we'll do that," I said eagerly. "Promise me."

"I promise," Lou replied. "We will."

Later I lay in the tent in the dark thinking about that promise, and I believed it. Lou and I were setting out on a beautiful life, and we were already making our dreams together.

In Vietnam:
Under the Shadow of the Almighty

I LEARNED to pray the year my brother joined the army. Richard and I had grown up like best friends, even though he was four years younger. In a town as small as Hollandale, you don't have many kids your age, and your siblings are important to you.

He started down the wrong path in high school, and when he got to Ole Miss, the wheels really began to fly off. He loved to party, and college gave him plenty of opportunities. By the end of his sophomore year, he recognized that his life was in turmoil. He had no direction, and he knew he had to make a drastic change.

Richard didn't register for classes his junior year, knowing full well what would happen. It was September 1968. The Vietnam War was raging—North Vietnam and the Viet Cong had launched the Tet Offensive earlier in the year—and Richard's college deferment was the only thing standing between him and active military duty. The draft board immediately reclassified him 1-A, available for military service. But before he could be enlisted in the infantry, he applied to officer candidate school and was accepted. They trained him to be a pilot, and he graduated as a second lieutenant infantry officer.

Before he shipped out, Richard married his college sweetheart, Dianne, and we all celebrated Christmas together. On January 1, 1969, he arrived in Vietnam and prepared for his first reconnaissance flight in what they called a "Bird Dog," a tiny, single-engine Cessna that could take off from a short runway then fly with low altitude and low speed. Richard flew less than a hundred feet above the jungle canopy, peering down to spot Viet Cong guerrillas or North Vietnamese soldiers. The enemy could have shot him down so easily—and the only reason they didn't was that shooting him meant identifying their own location.

When he found enemy soldiers, he radioed back for helicopter gunships or fighters. Then he dropped white phosphorus rockets to mark the target and got out as fast as he could, because at that point the VC had nothing to lose. They fired at him, and he prayed his armored seat and flak vest would protect him. Richard was so vulnerable in that little plane.

I had always prayed silently, but when Richard went to war, the burden was too great to keep my prayers in my head. I got on my knees and cried out to the Lord, and it totally revolutionized my communication with God. From that time on I never prayed silently again. I began reading scripture and praying it back to God. For Richard, I prayed Psalm 91.

Richard told me later about a night mission, when he had been in country for about two months. The jungle was totally black at night, and when clouds covered the moon and stars, the whole world was black. He had to rely on his instruments rather than his sight and instincts. He was thinking about where he was, where he had been, and where he was going. He had been in country long enough to see friends die, and he knew there was a good chance he might not come home alive. Completely alone,

Psalm 91

Whoever dwells in the shelter of the Most High
will rest in the shadow of the Almighty.
I will say of the LORD, *"He is my refuge*
and my fortress, my God, in whom I trust."

Surely he will save you
from the fowler's snare
and from the deadly pestilence.
He will cover you with his feathers,
and under his wings you will find refuge;
his faithfulness will be your shield and rampart.
You will not fear the terror of night,
nor the arrow that flies by day,
nor the pestilence that stalks in the darkness,
nor the plague that destroys at midday.
A thousand may fall at your side,
ten thousand at your right hand,
but it will not come near you.
You will only observe with your eyes
and see the punishment of the wicked.

*If you say, "The L*ORD *is my refuge,"*
  and you make the Most High your dwelling,
no harm will overtake you,
  no disaster will come near your tent.
For he will command his angels concerning you
  to guard you in all your ways;
they will lift you up in their hands,
  so that you will not strike your foot against a stone.
You will tread on the lion and the cobra;
  you will trample the great lion and the serpent.

*"Because he loves me," says the L*ORD, *"I will rescue*
him;
  I will protect him, for he acknowledges my name.
He will call on me, and I will answer him;
  I will be with him in trouble,
  I will deliver him and honor him.
With long life I will satisfy him
  and show him my salvation."

completely in the dark, he began to pray. "I hate to use a poker term," he would say later, "but I came to a point where I had to go all in. I prayed, 'Lord, if it's Your will, I want You to be my Lord and Savior.'" Richard points to that night as his "spiritual birth point."

All I knew at that point was that my brother was a world away, living the horrors of war in the jungle. I wrote him a letter every day. I guess I remembered my days as a kid at Camp Desoto, when Daddy wrote me every day. Daddy's letters meant so much, especially in the early days when I was so homesick. I wrote Richard every day for six months, and finally he wrote back, "Sis, I so enjoy your letters. I know this is not easy for you. But don't look at your letters as an assignment. You don't have to write every day."

I pictured the stack of letters, and it made me smile. I slowed down on the writing, but I continued to pray out loud for him every day. Then one day I recorded Psalm 91 on a cassette tape and mailed it to him. This was my prayer for Richard's protection.

I was learning what it was to cry out to God for something I wanted more than life itself—to see my brother come home whole, both mentally and physically.

Back in Mississippi my mother, father, and Dianne were on their knees too. We thought Richard would be coming home for Christmas the first year he was in Vietnam, but his orders were changed at the last minute. Mother postponed Christmas. "We'll have Christmas when Richard comes home," she said. Then she and Daddy kept the Christmas tree and the lights up until January. All the presents sat under the tree, still wrapped, for weeks. When Richard finally made it to Mississippi, we came together for the best Christmas we had ever experienced.

He had so many terrible stories of friends he had lost to enemy fire. One night the Viet Cong guerrillas had destroyed the entire village where he was staying, but he and others escaped.

Several times Dianne and my parents learned of attacks on what they believed were Richard's position. They would call me, and we would all pray, or I would drive to Mississippi and we would pray together. He was never wounded, and he had a powerful testimony of God's nearness in the midst of the unthinkable.

On his way home to Mississippi, Richard's flight landed in Oakland. As he stepped off the plane with two other men in uniform, a young woman ran up to the three of them. Unlike today, when we honor our men in uniform, this woman yelled, "You baby killers! Baby killers!" Those were the first words those three men heard—no welcome, no thank you. Instead they were told that they were terrible people doing terrible things.

My younger brother became my hero and, in many ways, a big brother to me for the rest of my life. At the moment when it appeared to me that all was lost in my own life, it was Richard who called—even though he had no idea how black my night had become. He understood what it meant to be under the shadow of the Almighty.

A Miracle Worker

LOU AND I were hoping for children, but several years after we married we were still just hoping. When I was a teenager and a college student, one of my deepest desires was to be a wife and mother, and now I had begun to get discouraged. My doctor ran tests and performed several minor procedures, none of which worked. Each month I wasn't pregnant became another letdown.

Then a friend told me about two fertility specialists who had the reputation of miracle workers: Dr. Abraham Velkoff and Dr. Jacob Epstein—Abraham and Jacob. Dr. Velkoff was the older of the two and had earned a great reputation in Atlanta. Lou and I discussed the possibility of my seeing them, and we agreed that I should. "But Lou," I said, "it might be very expensive."

"If they're that good," he said, "they'll be worth it." Plus, Lou was finishing his degree, and he would soon have better opportunities at the bank.

I was so nervous when I arrived at the office to see Dr. Velkoff.

"Let's just talk for a few minutes," he said, helping me to relax.

I gave him my big sob story about how we had done this and done that and we still didn't have a baby. "My heart's desire is to have a child," I explained, "and I'm glad to be able to see you."

"I'd like to help you," he said. "The first thing I need to do is examine you."

After his examination he said, "Well, Mrs. Sulcer, I have news for you. You're pregnant."

"Are you sure?" I asked. "I mean, it can't be. I didn't think it was possible."

"I know my business pretty well, Mrs. Sulcer," he said, "but if it will make you feel better, I'll run a test. My office will call you tomorrow with the results."

I ran out of his office and found a pay phone in the parking lot to call Lou at the bank.

"You're not going to believe this!" I exclaimed. "I'm pregnant!"

"Wow!" Lou said. "That guy really is a miracle worker."

Super Lou

WHEN OUR baby girl, Christy, was nine months old, we bought our first little home and moved from Roswell Court to Marietta. As soon as we were settled in, we joined Eastside Baptist Church. Lou hated the spotlight, and yet somehow the spotlight seemed to find him. He would have avoided walking down the aisle and our introduction to the church if it had been possible. But that was part of the process. On that Sunday morning we stood in front of the congregation, and the pastor announced that not only were we the newest members of the church, but that Lou was the one thousandth member of Eastside Baptist Church. They made a huge deal about it and put our picture in the *Marietta Daily Journal*.

"Why couldn't we have joined last week?" Lou said. "We could have been number 999."

WHEN LOU and I met, everybody called him Louie. In fact, his high school friends and his sister and brother-in-law still call him Louie. But when we moved to Marietta and joined Eastside Baptist Church, Louie became Lou almost overnight.

The church at that time was too small to have a youth pastor, and they didn't have much going on Sunday nights except the church service. Lou suggested we invite the kids to our house on Sunday nights. Lou connected with those teenagers at their level and interests. We were young, of course, still in our twenties, and Lou was an athlete. The fact that he had played football at Tech, and he was still bigger, faster, and stronger than any of the boys who came to the house, gave him instant credibility. He could beat them at any game they wanted to play. His love for those kids and his willingness to show it added to his charisma. One of the boys called him "Super Lou," and the nickname stuck. In our house, he was never Louie again.

The first Sunday night we had eight or ten kids, and a week later there were a dozen. Soon the group was outgrowing our house. I had seen the power of Campus Crusade and invited a young man to lead a Bible study for the teenagers at our house.

In the afternoon before the kids came, Lou would move the furniture out of the living room, and soon the room would fill up, with kids spilling out onto the front stoop. Several brought guitars, and sometimes our neighbors would sit on their porches and listen. Not that the kids sang so well—they were simply full of joy.

Lou became a Sunday school teacher for high school junior boys, and the experience and preparation for teaching every week opened his heart more to spiritual growth. He followed a curriculum, but one night he told me, "These lessons aren't speaking to where the boys are. I have to get it down to their level." The kids respected and admired Lou, and so did their parents. He was nominated and ordained as a deacon. Later the pastor asked him to help manage the church finances (they didn't have a business manager at the time), and Lou would stop at Eastside on his way home from the bank. He was pouring everything he had into the church.

The Most Bittersweet of Times

THE MORNING Andrea was born, Lou's mother had a heart attack. I was in maternity at Northside Hospital, and Ruth was up in the intensive care unit. Andrea and I went home, but Ruth remained for sixteen days until she passed away. Lou and his sister, Linda, took turns staying with their mother; Lou took days, and Linda took nights. That left me at home with a toddler and a newborn. If you're looking for the definition of a bittersweet time, that was it. Mother came over from Mississippi to help me.

Christmas was two months later, and when I asked Lou where he wanted to spend the holidays, he said, "We're going home. To Hollandale."

The Gift of a Son

LOU LOVED our girls so much, and yet I knew he wanted a son. He never voiced that, but I knew. When we were expecting our third child, I wanted so much for it to be a boy. I went into labor, and when Lou was driving me to the hospital, the Lord dropped into my spirit: "I'm about to give you a son."

The feeling was so sudden and so clear, I had to catch myself from answering out loud. In all my life I had never experienced such a clear expression into my heart. And yet I was afraid to tell Lou.

Later in the delivery room I had an epidural block, so I was fully awake yet pain free. At the moment of delivery, the doctor smiled and said, "This has to be a girl. She's too beautiful to be a boy."

"No," I said, "it can't be."

I wasn't so much disappointed as surprised.

"Whoops," the doctor said. "It is a boy. How'd you know that?"

I couldn't say, "God told me on the way." Instead I just smiled. But I was certain then that I had heard the voice of the Holy Spirit in the car, and I knew what that voice felt like.

At Home for Sunday Dinner

SOMETIMES YOU just want to go home, not the home where you live with your spouse and children, but home where your mother takes care of you. Home where you're safe and protected. That's the way I felt one Sunday after church. I was standing at the kitchen counter making bologna or peanut butter sandwiches for Lou and the children, and I was homesick for Sunday dinner at our house in Hollandale, Mississippi.

It never occurred to my mother to throw together sandwiches after church. Instead she started preparing Sunday dinner on Saturday afternoon and finished on Sunday, and we sat down to a proper meal around the table—fried chicken, fresh beans and tomatoes from the garden, cornbread, pie for dessert. We sat at the table every night for supper, but Sunday dinner was different. We didn't have any Sunday afternoon activities to run off to, so we never rushed through dinner. Sometimes our pastor and his wife joined us, or we might have friends at the table with us, and we just relaxed in each other's company. Those were important times for me as a child.

Now I stood at the kitchen counter, reminiscing about those long, slow Sundays back home. A week later those same thoughts filled my head and weighed down my heart, and when I felt homesick the third Sunday in a row, I thought, *I'm never going home to Mother for Sunday dinner*. But if that was such a special time for me growing up, why not make it important to my family?

The next Sunday morning, I stopped feeling sorry for myself. I woke up early and put a roast in the oven. Lou smelled it cooking and came into the kitchen.

"What are you doing?" he asked.

"I'm fixing Sunday dinner. We're coming home from church today and eating in the dining room."

"Well, okay," he said, and his indifference didn't bother me a bit.

That Sunday we came home from church, and we all sat around the table and talked—no kitchen chaos slapping together sandwiches—and Lou loved it most of all. He enjoyed anything that brought our children together. The camaraderie and joy he shared with Christy, Andrea, and Kevin mattered most to him.

From that day forward Sunday dinner became a highlight of our week, an anchor for our family that we knew we could count on wherever we lived, whatever was going on around us. Week after week, year after year, we had a safe place to come to on Sunday. Later I read a book by Edith Schaeffer where she wrote about establishing family traditions and that it's important for children to say, "We always do this."

We always sat down to Sunday dinner.

Growing . . . Apart

SOON AFTER we joined Eastside Baptist Church, Lou and I were both teaching Sunday school classes. Through our teaching we were growing in our own knowledge, but not together as a couple.

For Christmas one year I asked Lou for *Vine's Complete Expository Dictionary of Old and New Testament Words*. My life revolved around the Bible. Every night after I put the children to sleep, and while Lou was watching TV in the other room, I sat on our bed surrounded by Bible commentaries and books, eager to grow and learn about becoming a godly wife and building a Christian home. I couldn't get enough of it, like a seminary student. Other women were hooked on soap operas; I was hooked on *Back to the Bible*. I timed our children's naps around the radio show every day.

Whenever a Bible study was announced, I signed up for it, as long as a nursery was available. When Bill Gothard brought his weeklong seminar to Atlanta, I registered us. Every night for a week Lou and I joined thousands of others in the Omni Coliseum listening to the teaching.

The church sponsored a couples' retreat, but Lou didn't want to go. He enjoyed mentoring teenage boys, but he had an almost overwhelming fear of speaking in public. I, on the other hand, loved speaking in front of people. I thought if we could only create opportunities for Lou to speak out, he would enjoy it the same way I did. A couples' retreat might be the place to start.

So I told him, "I know what I want for my birthday. I want for you and me to go to the couples retreat."

Lou had an almost pained look on his face, and he said, "No, I would rather not."

I pushed harder. "You wouldn't even go for my birthday?"

"I just don't want to do that, Harriet," he said.

I let that become a wound that I held on to.

Today I tell young wives that they can have a couple's retreat every night in their home. Close the commentaries and go to the other room to be with your husband. That's how you become a godly wife. That's how you build a Christian family.

Priorities

I WAS WAY too busy early in our marriage doing things that didn't mean a hill of beans. Lou's mother came to the house and said, "You could eat off these floors."

I smiled proudly.

Yes, I thought, they're spotless.

You couldn't find a speck of dust in our home. I was a fanatical housekeeper, all the time not realizing that Lou could not have cared less. He just needed my attention.

To the Farm

LOU WAS suffocating in his job, and I had no idea until he wound up in the hospital. At first it was hypoglycemia, which his doctor said was stress related. Then he had chest pains, and we thought he was having a heart attack. That's when his doctor told him to think about leaving the bank. Lou didn't have the temperament or the desire for the corporate world. He would come home, pull off his tie, and tell me, "It's so political down there." He was not interested in climbing the corporate ladder. But I was wrapped up in our three small children, and I didn't understand how bad it was for him.

Then a friend of Lou's from high school who was in the real estate business offered a lifeline, and Lou took it. He went to work selling farms in north Georgia, many of them chicken farms, and soon he was dreaming of country living. A few months later Lou said he wanted to take us on a ride to north Georgia.

"I need you to keep an open mind on this," Lou said.

We were driving out I-85 in the late afternoon, miles beyond the traffic of the Atlanta rush hour. Christy, Andrea, and Kevin were in the backseat, patient so far.

"Lou, why do you keep saying that?" I asked. "What do you mean?"

"I just want you to look at it and see what you think."

"It" was a piece of property out in the country. Lou had learned about it at the bank and had apparently driven out already and fallen in love. He came home and got us all in the car to show us. Almost an hour later, we were still driving up the interstate. Finally Lou said, "Here's the exit."

The sign read "Braselton." I had never heard of Braselton, but Lou drove down a two-lane road for a mile or so, and we were there—a pretty little town like the smallest towns out in the Delta of my childhood. Some brick storefronts, lovely homes, and a crossroads. Then just like that, we were out the other side, with rolling hills and pastures on both sides of the road. Lou turned onto a gravel driveway that wound its way toward a pretty farmhouse on a hill, and I knew he was right. This was a stunningly beautiful piece of property. But there was no way we could afford to buy it.

He parked the car in front of the house, and the late-afternoon sun was reflecting off the metal roofs of six long chicken houses across the road. We all got out of the car, and when the doors slammed shut, there was a moment of total silence—not like the quiet of the suburbs. This was country quiet—something altogether different. Then a mourning dove called from way off. We all stood and just looked around.

"It's really beautiful," I said.

"I hoped you'd like it," he said.

Andrea walked over, stood beside me, and took my hand. "But Lou," I said, "we can't afford to buy this."

"We can if we move up here," he said, and I suddenly knew what he was proposing.

I squeezed Andrea's little hand and caught a tiny scream in the back of my throat. The first words that came to mind were, "You want to move here?" But somehow I kept from saying anything. Lou must not have seen the shock, because he said, "Harriet, I want to bring our family up to this farm."

"You would leave Marietta?" I asked. "The real estate job?"

"I can sell real estate from here," he said. "It's even better. I'm closer to the farmland. Remember, I asked you to keep an open mind."

Most of the farmers relied on chickens for supplemental income in addition to their regular jobs. Lou would open a real estate office in Braselton and raise chickens at home.

"Lou, I just don't know."

But he had already decided. I could see it in his eyes and hear it in his voice. We were moving to the country.

✝ ✝ ✝

FOR DAYS before the move, Lou and I packed boxes. Christy was seven, and she could help some, but not so much Andrea and Kevin, who were four and two. Then one by one, the children started coughing, developed fevers, and lost their appetite. Lou and I were still packing silverware and plates, pictures and books—all sorts of small things that had been left to the very end—and I held my tears. In the middle of all that Kevin came into the living room saying his stomach itched.

"Show me your tummy," I said.

He lifted up his pajamas, and he was covered with red spots. Chickenpox. Within an hour Christy and Andrea came in with the same symptoms. One by one I put them in a lukewarm bath with a little cornstarch, then started in with the calamine lotion.

I put them to bed early, hoping they could sleep through some of the discomfort. I sat on the edge of Andrea's bed, and after she had said her prayers, she asked, "Mommy, do we have chicken-pox because we're moving to a chicken farm?"

I woke up the next morning heartsick and knew I needed help with the children, so I called my mother. "Can you come?" I asked. "I can't make it by myself."

Oh, Lord, Is This What You Want?

LOU HADN'T been trained to raise chickens. He had been a banker and a real estate agent. He had grown up in the city and spent the first decade of his career driving to work in a high-rise office building in the heart of Atlanta. But he visited with neighboring farmers to learn all he could about raising broilers and had several lengthy conversations with the former owner of the farm. He was confident and so was I. Lou was one of those men with an innate ability to repair a car engine, wire a house, or ride a horse. He could raise chickens. Of course, I didn't know anything. On our first morning in our new life, my mother hadn't arrived yet, but sixty thousand baby chicks were on the way. The trucks would arrive before noon. I woke up early and cooked a big breakfast for Lou. I stepped out the back door with him when he walked across the yard to work, and the beauty of the place almost overwhelmed me. Once again I was struck by how quiet it was and how far I could see to the horizon. This truly was God's creation, and I thanked Him for allowing me to experience it.

I went back inside to take care of the children, and an hour or so later the truck rumbled up the driveway with the baby chicks. Mother had not yet arrived, so I watched from the window with Christy, Andrea, and Kevin as the trucks backed up and men hauled big boxes from the trailer into the chicken houses. Mother came in the late afternoon, so the next morning I would be able to help Lou.

At breakfast I asked Lou, "So what will we be doing today?"

"This is the hardest time," he said, "when they're chicks. They call them poults, and you have to feed them by hand."

"By hand!" I cried. "Lou, we can't feed sixty thousand chickens by hand. It's not possible!"

I thought he meant the way you feed other baby animals by hand, with a dropper. I was glad Mother hadn't come into the kitchen yet.

"No, not literally by hand," he said.

"But that's what you said. 'By hand.' Lou, I don't think this is going to work."

"It'll be okay. You just walk through the house with a bucket of feed and scoop it into the feeding trough where they can get it. In a few days they'll be big enough to reach the automatic feeder."

Lou ate and went straight out to the chicken houses while I put on a little matching shorts outfit that I thought would work for the farmer's wife. I was determined to put the best face on the day.

Then I walked across the yard and opened the door to the first house, and the sound of ten thousand peeping little chicks almost overwhelmed me. They were so loud. All those thousands of yellow puffs, just like Easter chicks, all around my feet, all over the gigantic house, all peeping at the same time. Lou was at the other end, nearly four hundred feet away, and he hadn't seen me come in.

"Lou," I called out trying to sound cheerful, "what do you want me to do?"

He didn't hear me over the chicks, so I called louder, "Lou!"

He looked up.

"What do you want me to do?" I yelled.

"See that bucket by the door?" he yelled back.

I reached over and picked up the tin bucket. It looked good for carrying feed. "This one?"

"Yes," he said. "You need to walk to this end of the house and put all the dead chickens in that bucket."

The horror of the instructions swept over me, and I dropped the bucket with a clank. Chicks scattered. I looked back at Lou, but he had already turned his back and moved on to another chore. I looked down at the bucket, and a dead chick lay beside it. I hadn't killed it. I just hadn't seen it. It was bloody, like it had been pecked. I picked the chick up by the toe with two fingers and dropped it into the bottom of the bucket, then looked down at it. One dead baby chicken lying in a bucket.

"You've got to be kidding," I said plenty loud, but not loud enough for Lou to hear over all those chickens. "This cannot be my life."

Then I watched him walk out the back door to go to the next house, and I wept. I wanted to sit down and curl up, but the dirt floor was covered with chicken poop. I dropped the bucket again and looked up toward the tin roof. "Oh, Lord, is this what you want from me?" I cried. "Is it? Really?"

He didn't answer. There were only ten thousand chickens peeping. So I picked up the bucket and started walking—sort of shuffling, actually, so I wouldn't step on a chick and kill it. I hadn't gone far when I saw another little yellow ball of fluff on its back, feet up. How many would there be?

I looked toward the back door and yelled, "Lou Sulcer, I can't believe you've done this! I'm a college graduate, and you've got me picking up dead chickens!"

But Lou was gone, and I was alone with the chickens. I kept shuffling, crying harder with every dead chick. Before long I had a yellow pile of a dozen of them. And this was just the first house.

Finally out the back door, I found Lou standing between the first two houses. I took a deep breath to keep from crying more, but I didn't wipe my tears with my filthy hands. He turned around. "What do I do with them?" I asked, barely masking my disgust.

"Toss them in that pit over there," he said. "I'll put some lime over them and bury them."

I don't remember how many more hours I spent picking up dead chickens and throwing them into the pit before I went to the house where Mother was fixing lunch. I rinsed off and tried to look my best. I couldn't tell her what I had been doing. "Helping Lou," was all I would tell her. After a few days the children were better, and early the next morning, I watched Mother drive away. I longed to scoop up the children and run after her. We could go home to Mississippi while Lou got his chicken farm up and going. She and Daddy could take care of us for a few weeks until school started. But she turned onto the road, and I watched until she was out of sight.

Lou had assured me once again that the hardest part of the chicken business was when the chicks were young. This would pass soon. In the meantime, though, he worked hard, day and night. This was nothing like what I remembered from the farmers back home. They hired men to work the farm. But we didn't have money for Lou to hire help. That would come with the success of our first flock.

Sleeping in the Car

ONE NIGHT after Mother left, Lou needed my help. We couldn't leave the children in the house alone, so I got them bathed and dressed for bed, then we gathered up books and pallets. They brought everything out and climbed into the station wagon, and I drove down and parked right outside the chicken houses. They loved it! They were happy and Lou was happy.

Pebbles for Goats

WE ALSO had a herd of goats. Well, actually the goats belonged to the pastor at Mount Zion Baptist Church, but we were taking care of them. Every day Pastor John came by and milked those goats. I didn't milk goats. I had to draw the line somewhere.

We learned by experience that goats will climb onto anything. When we got in the pickup truck, they jumped into the bed and rode around in the back. One day Lou parked the station wagon outside the chicken houses, and one of the goats hopped over and climbed onto the hood, slipping and sliding on the hood and scratching the paint before Lou yelled and scared it off. So from that day on, Kevin, who was three years old, had a job that he took very seriously. I put him on the hood of the car and gave him a little pile of rocks. If a goat was about to climb up on the car, Kevin would throw one of those little pebbles at it.

At Home in the Woods

MOTHER AND Daddy came to visit us at the farm a few months after we had bought it, and Daddy was not impressed. His son-in-law, the banker, had become a chicken farmer. Not only that, but the farm had not even modernized. It looked like a money pit. To Daddy, the idea was as crazy as the old TV comedy *Green Acres*, where a successful New York lawyer buys a farm and drags his glamorous Hungarian wife to live with him out in the country. He never came right out and said it, but Lou and I could both read his body language. His daughter should not be working in a chicken house.

Daddy and Lou would never fully understand each other's point of view. Once we were visiting my parents in Hollandale, and Daddy invited Lou to join him at the Rotary Club meeting. Daddy was active in Rotary International and had visited clubs all over Central America. He enjoyed few things more than meeting and getting to know new people, and was sure Lou must think the same way. But Lou said he wanted to relax that day—we were on vacation—and maybe take the children fishing on the creek bank. Daddy just shook his head.

Where Daddy and Lou did connect was in the woods.

The farm was close to the north Georgia mountains, and whenever we could get away on a Friday afternoon, we drove up and pitched a tent, sometimes near Unicoi Gap or over the mountain closer to Hiawassee or down at Vogel State Park. We had some favorite places, but we also enjoyed exploring.

My brother and I had grown up camping with our parents, and long after we had left home, Mother and Daddy were still pitching a tent in the woods. Every morning Mother cooked bacon and eggs or pancakes in a pan over an open fire. For dinner she worked magic with tinfoil and hot coals.

Later they bought a motor home, and their tent camping days were over. For the next decade they traveled from Florida to the Pocono Mountains. And they always came through Georgia.

On neutral ground in the outdoors, which they both loved, Daddy and Lou found their bond. Lou was the father of Daddy's grandchildren, and they both had limitless supplies of love for Christy, Andrea, and Kevin. When children were around, they were the center of the two men's attention and the topic of their conversation.

We built a fire every night and sat with the children on our laps, reminiscing about campfires a generation ago, or Mother and Daddy might tell stories of their childhood. I shared our dream of building a cabin in the woods someday. The children started nodding off, and we carried them to the tent and put them in their sleeping bag, and in the morning we started all over again with the wonderful smell of wood smoke and bacon frying.

Encouragers, Just in Time

GOD SENT help to the farm before we even knew what to ask for: encouragement before we grew weary. Darius Kilpatrick called and said he was coming up to the farm on Saturday, and he was bringing a tractor and plow. He and Juda, his wife, and their teenage sons were going to help us put in our garden. (I hadn't planned a garden!)

Darius and Juda had become our good friends at Eastside Baptist. They were a few years older than we and were a farm couple at heart, even though they lived in suburban Marietta and he worked for General Motors. Darius totally believed in the farm so much that he bought the tractor and left it for us to use any time.

But he went way overboard on the garden. When you plow your garden with a walk-behind tiller, you get worn out quickly, and you tend to set your sights lower. But sitting up on that tractor and pulling a plow behind it, Darius could have plowed five acres before lunchtime without breaking a sweat. As it was, he plowed a garden big enough to support twelve families. We planted long rows of corn, beans, okra, and tomatoes. We made hills for planting cantaloupe, watermelon, and squash.

At the end of the day we went into the house, and standing in the kitchen, Juda wanted to make sure I was ready for the harvest to come.

"Where's your pressure cooker?" she asked.

"I don't have a pressure cooker."

"You don't have a pressure cooker?" She was polite but incredulous.

"No, I don't."

"Well, we have to have one."

I had grown up watching my mother work in the vegetable garden and had helped her in the kitchen canning vegetables and making preserves. But canning had never interested me like cooking and baking. Juda came the next weekend with a pressure cooker and dozens of jars. I thought, *This is not the way I want to spend my summer.*

On weekday mornings Lou got out to the chickens early and walked through all the houses checking food and water, cleaning up, and repairing anything that might have broken. By the time he came back in, the children were up and I had baked homemade muffins and cooked bacon and scrambled eggs. Some mornings I made oatmeal, which I cooked with whole milk slowly over a double boiler. Never cereal from a box. I wanted my family to have a good nutritious breakfast. Lou needed nutrition as much as the children. He was pushing so hard. But he never sat down to breakfast. Instead he grabbed a muffin and poured a cup of coffee, then headed over to Braselton, where he was fixing up a mobile home for his real estate office.

The Kilpatricks came up the next Saturday, and while Darius worked with Lou, Juda and I turned a downstairs playroom into a little schoolroom for Christy, Andrea, and Kevin. Juda had taught at the Eastside kindergarten for years, and I had taught second grade. I think we enjoyed creating that space as much as the children did playing in it.

My tendency in those days was to worry, and when the twenty-year-old son of one of our neighbors was electrocuted after falling across a feeder with faulty wiring, I grew fearful for Lou. He came home from the office and went out to the chickens after dinner almost every night. The plan had been for him to hire help on the farm so he could focus on his day job, but that never worked out. His hires wouldn't show up or would move on without notice. The chicken houses were a quarter-mile from our house, too far to look out the window and see Lou if he was inside. So I asked him to buy walkie-talkies so we could communicate.

Then something magical happened. The Kilpatricks' sons had gone back to Eastside Baptist and told the other kids how much fun Saturdays were on Super Lou's farm. A week later the youth director came driving up in the church bus filled with teenagers eager to work in the garden and the chicken houses. Immediately we became a satellite gathering place for the youth. Almost every Saturday a carload of teenage boys made their way up to work on the farm. Sometimes they brought a whole busload.

Some of the Eastside youth had graduated and were students at the University of Georgia, just thirty miles away. They heard what was going on and drove over to visit and work with us. We constantly had teenagers and college kids in and out of the house, and Lou loved it. He fired up two or three grills to make sure there was plenty of food for everybody. Then at night we built a bonfire, and a couple of the guys brought out guitars. Our children hung on every word the "big kids" spoke and sang. They learned "Pass It On" and "He's Everything to Me" and a dozen other songs around those campfires.

In late summer more friends, Frank and Shirley McDaniel, asked if they could spend their vacation camping down by the creek. Of course we said yes, and they also quickly fell into the farm routine, with Frank helping Lou with the chickens and Shirley working with me, canning in the kitchen.

So many things went right for us at the farm. The children loved living out in the country, and they loved the hard work. I had thought we would completely lose touch with our friends at Eastside Baptist, sixty miles away, but we actually grew closer than ever to the Kilpatricks and others.

Honeysuckle Dreams

I GREW TO love that farm, waking up before the sun and listening to the world come alive on dewy mornings. As the sun rose I could enjoy a quiet time, praying for Lou and the children and journaling. One of my favorite sights was of Lou on the tractor, cutting hay. He looked so alive.

For my birthday I asked for a bicycle, and Lou put a carrier on the back for Kevin to sit in. We rode out the driveway and across the road to the garden, where I worked until the day grew too hot. Or sometimes in the morning I just put him in that little seat and rode all over those country roads, singing "Pass It On" all the way. His clear soprano voice sang out behind me, "It only takes a spark . . ."

One morning I wrote my parents a note, "The whole world smells like honeysuckle!" Everywhere Kevin and I rode, the fencerows swelled with blooming honeysuckle vines, sweetening the morning air.

There was a small Christian school for kindergarten through fifth grade close by, Jackson Trail Christian Academy. It was like something out of *Little House on the Prairie*. I loved the idea of Christian education with strong academics, and we enrolled Christy and Andrea there in the fall. It didn't take us long to realize we weren't going to pay for private school with the chicken farm and Lou's real estate business, so when the school had an opening, I went back to teaching. Kevin started kindergarten, and we all rode to school together.

I taught second and third graders, and on days when the students finished all their work, we went on an adventure—usually down to a creek that ran through the property. We took several big quilts, spread out, and ate lunch. Then the children would lie down and rest, and I would read a book. Those were sweet, sweet times.

I supplemented my teaching salary by driving the school bus every day, taking that big yellow bus up and around all those county roads to pick up children, and driving them home in the afternoon. Every night that old bus was parked in our yard. That was country living!

Lou devoted himself to our children, and they responded with their love. There was a farm pond behind the chicken houses, and Lou and Andrea spent hours back there catching fish. Fishing had been a big deal in Lou's family. His mother and his Aunt Moddie would drive up to Lake Allatoona, where they fished and smoked Marlboros until late in the afternoon. Then they drove back to town, fried up platters of fish, and served them on the back screen porch with tomatoes from the garden.

But even more important than fishing for Lou was football, the game he excelled at in high school and loved all his life. He saw athletic talent in Kevin early, and he planned to help him make the most of it.

Our girls were going to summer camp with our church group, and there was a spot for Kevin in the children's camp. All of the other rising second-grade children were going, and it would be a wonderful week for him.

I was also excited because in five years on the farm, Lou and I hadn't had any time away together, just the two of us. We didn't take a family vacation the entire time, and we never scheduled date nights or moments for just the two of us. I wanted so badly for us to have that week together without the children.

"Kevin can't go," Lou said. "He has football camp that week."

"But Lou," I said, "he just finished first grade. Football camp?"

Lou insisted. If Kevin was going to be an athlete, he had to start young.

I wanted Lou's attention, and I resented him for his decision, though I didn't tell him so. I tucked that wound inside.

In the meantime, our farm operation was hindered by aging equipment and wasn't generating the income we had expected. Lou's real estate business was hit hard by rising interest rates in the 1970s—people simply couldn't afford to pay double-digit interest on a farm loan—and sales didn't materialize. We needed more income to pay the bills, so I joined our friend Jackie Beavers selling cosmetics and began building a team on the phone in the evenings.

To deal with the stress, Lou started waking up early and running every morning. Christy admired her father so much, she asked if she could run with him. I didn't realize what was happening to Lou personally. The farm was his dream, and now the dream was dying. No matter how hard he worked, those broilers would grow only so fast, and Lou could sell them for only so much. When the chicken processing company starting pressuring Lou to modernize the houses for better production, we just couldn't do it. The investment would have required another loan, and we were on such a tight budget we were barely surviving.

The cosmetics sales were going so well, however, the company offered us the chance to run a distribution center in Athens, Georgia. We had to take it. We sold the farm to a neighbor who wanted to expand his operation, breathing a sigh of relief and never taking time to mourn the loss. Lou had been at his best when we went to the country, and our first years on the farm had been the happiest and healthiest of our married life. Now, without our realizing it, the downward spiral was beginning.

Snow Days!

LIVING CLOSER to Athens, home of the University of Georgia, Lou and I reconnected with students we had grown to love in the youth group years earlier in Marietta. That winter a snowstorm was coming, and I went to the grocery store to stock up. Two of the kids were there, and of course we started talking about the weather.

"Can we come to your house?" Kathy asked.

"What do you mean?" I said.

"We want to get snowed in at your house," Beaver said.

I could hardly believe it. Here were two college students whose idea of a house party on a snow day was with a family of five from their church.

I laughed and said, "Well, okay. Let me get some more food."

"We'll bring food," Kathy said.

The snow started that afternoon, and by nightfall we had six college students with their sleeping bags in our living room. The next morning we were truly snowed in. I made pots of chili while the college kids and our children made snowmen and played outside. We had three joyful days before the roads were cleared and the university opened.

A Young Evangelist

WE WERE AT Sunday night service one week sitting near the front, and Kevin had his head on my lap. The girls were sitting on my other side. At the end of the service the pastor gave an invitation to commit your life to Christ. Kevin sat up and told me, "I want to go forward."

"Not tonight, honey," I said. "Let's wait."

I thought he hadn't heard a word all night—that he didn't know what he was doing.

"No," he said, "I want to go now. "

But I wouldn't let him. "Let's wait until the service is over so you can talk to the pastor."

When most everyone had left, we went up and I told the pastor, "Kevin really wanted to come forward when you gave the invitation tonight. I'd like for you to talk with him before he does this."

He took Kevin to his office, and after about thirty minutes they came out. The pastor told me, "You let him come. I haven't talked to many adults who are as ready as this child is."

The next Sunday night Kevin went forward and was baptized, and it was like he was instantly on fire for the Lord. All three of our children were memorizing Bible verses. Kevin had so much of the Word in him at a young age, he became like a little evangelist. We had a Good News glove, a multicolored glove that

Child Evangelism Fellowship distributes to help children understand the gospel and basic biblical truths. Kevin's friend Ramar, who was Muslim, was over one day, and they were playing with Legos in Kevin's room. I was working on laundry, and when I took Kevin's clean clothes to his room, he was wearing that glove and pointing to the black finger. Ramar was watching him closely.

"Now, this one is sin," Kevin said. "Do you know what sin is?"

"No," Ramar said.

I didn't say anything, but just eased out of the room. "Lord, I don't know where he's going with this," I prayed quietly, "just please help him."

A few years later, Kevin invited a friend to spend the night during the week of vacation Bible school. He wanted to take Mark to VBS the next day. While I was cooking dinner, Kevin came down to the kitchen and said calmly, "Mom, Mark is ready to accept Christ. Can you come up and help us?"

I dropped a dish on the counter with a clank and asked, "What's going on, honey?"

"I've been telling him about Jesus," he said, "and I'd feel better if you came up and helped."

I went up and talked with Mark, and he said he was absolutely ready to receive Christ. So the next morning Mark went with Kevin to vacation Bible school and told the teacher he had prayed to receive Christ the night before. The teacher visited with me, and the next Sunday, Mark's whole family came to church for him to be baptized.

That's where Kevin was at eleven years old. He had such a tender heart.

Children First. Always.

THE COSMETICS company expanded into Mississippi and wanted Lou and me to oversee the operation for the entire state.

It was a great opportunity, like a homecoming for me.

We moved to Jackson, and Lou ran the distribution center while I started calling people I knew and building a sales team. We worked hard on the business, but our hearts were somewhere else. Lou made a place for himself in the sports program at Jackson Academy, where our children attended. He coached football for sixth and seventh graders, and the other fathers loved him. They didn't do anything but win, and Lou always had a positive influence on boys he coached. Kevin played on his team and excelled. He also started tae kwon do, a journey that would take him to a black belt and a national championship.

The move to Jackson was hard on Christy, who was in ninth grade, a difficult age to ask a child to pull up stakes. But it didn't take her long to find her way. She was an athlete, still running after her years on the farm with Lou, and she was selected for the school dance team.

Lou and I poured everything into Christy, Andrea, and Kevin. We enrolled them in the best private school in Jackson, despite our limited financial resources. Lou never missed his football team's practices, and they won year after year. I was the mom who drove the cheerleaders or the drill team wherever they needed to go. Our home was a gathering spot for our children's friends.

Even when we needed each other, we put the children first. I was lying in a hospital bed recovering from surgery, not life threatening but the pain was almost unbearable. Lou came into the room, and I was so happy to see him. He sat for a while and neither of us said much. I was just trying to keep from crying.

Then he said, "I can't stay too long. Kevin's game starts in an hour."

"Oh, honey," I said, "please stay with me. My legs are aching so bad. Can't the other coaches take care of it?"

Then, as hard as I tried not to, I started to cry. Lou hated when I cried. He either felt guilty or thought I was trying to manipulate him. When I cried, he got frustrated and angry, and any sympathy he might have felt for me drained away. I cried, and he left for the football game.

We didn't mean to hurt each other, but if Christy or Andrea or Kevin needed one of us, they got first priority, no matter what.

Mimi: A Tree-Climbing Grandmother

MOVING TO Jackson meant living ninety miles from my parents—a wonderful treat for the children and me. My mother may have worn white gloves and been president of the garden club, but at heart she was a country girl—never more so than after she became a grandmother.

One day when we were visiting Mother and Daddy, I was in the kitchen while she was dressing for garden club—high heels and a dress, of course, plus a hat and white gloves. The children were outside playing, and Andrea was climbing the magnolia tree in the front yard.

Mother stepped out the door, and my brother's children, who were also visiting, were all upset. Andrea had climbed so high in the tree, she was afraid to come down. Mother hurried around the house and quickly sized up the situation. Andrea was crying and afraid.

"It's okay," Mother said. "We'll get you down."

Then she kicked off her high-heel shoes, pulled off her gloves, and started up the tree. There was a gap in the foliage just below the spot where Andrea was sitting, and Mother could look through it across the street to Deer Creek. She might have stayed there with her granddaughter if she hadn't had a meeting to attend.

About that time a car came down the street and slowed down. It was one of Mother's friends from garden club.

"Hey, Ida Mae," Mother called, as if climbing a magnolia tree in a dress was something she did every day.

"Hey, Harriet," Ida Mae replied, and she drove on.

Mother calmed Andrea enough to get her down from the tree, brushed her hands together, then put on her shoes and gloves and drove on to her meeting.

Hard Times in Mississippi

AS IT TURNED out, living in Mississippi increased the distance between my parents and Lou. Because of our financial struggles, Daddy assumed Lou was not working hard enough to support us. In fact, Lou worked amazingly hard at everything he did.

Mother and Daddy drove up for a visit, and Lou was home when they arrived. I came home from the distribution center a little while later, and when I opened the door, Daddy jumped up from his chair and exclaimed, "There's my working girl!"

That cut Lou deep. We all knew what Daddy was saying. His subtleties were rarely subtle.

When the cosmetics business didn't take off as we had hoped, Lou started looking for other possibilities. The father of one of Lou's players was a homebuilder, and he offered Lou a job over-seeing the construction of a new home in Summertree, an up-scale development north of Jackson. Rather than pay Lou a salary, he offered him a percentage of the sales price, which would mean more money in the end.

Always the perfectionist, Lou took great pride in that house, like it was his own. Some days he was swinging a hammer him-self, making sure the project stayed on schedule.

His hips had started hurting him, though, and the pain in-creased to the point that some days he had a hard time getting out of bed. He had pushed himself so hard on the farm those years, plus he had an undiagnosed chronic disease, lupus, which can cause deterioration of the hip. The orthopedic surgeon told him both hips would have to be replaced. Lou wanted to wait until the house was completed, but the surgeon said sooner was better—first one hip, then the other.

While he was in the hospital, the homebuilder declared bankruptcy. Lou never saw it coming. He lost his job, the promise of any income from his months of work on the house, and his medical benefits in one awful blow.

Without medical benefits, the bills from the follow-up to Lou's surgery grew quickly. The cosmetics business would never generate enough income to keep up. Plus, Christy was starting college. Lou had to find a job fast. Our financial hope was back in Atlanta, where he had friends and potential contacts. He was fifty years old, depressed, and still on crutches, recovering from his hip replacements, on the day he drove away from Jackson. He said he would find a job and a place to live, then we could follow.

It would have been so easy for us to stay in Mississippi. Christy, Andrea, and Kevin had all done great in school. Asking Andrea and Kevin to pull up roots again almost seemed cruel. But we didn't have a choice without breaking up the family.

Lou called a few days later to tell us he had found a job and a house to rent, but he said not to come yet. It was a sales job with a friend who owned an export company, and he needed to get his feet on the ground a little more firmly. Maybe we should stay in Mississippi for a few weeks.

"Of course we're coming," I said.

Something about the way he vaguely said, "Maybe in a few weeks" gave me the impression that it might stretch into a few months.

"We have to go through this together, Lou," I said.

There was silence from the other end.

"Yeah," he said. "I guess you're right.

In hindsight, I see the toll that the farm and the hip replacements had taken on Lou. He was no longer Super Lou. He had been one of the strongest men you would ever meet—a natural athlete. When all else failed, he could do anything he wanted physically and athletically. Suddenly at age fifty he couldn't do any of that. He had lost his identity. Plus, both of his parents had died when they were fifty-two, and though he never said it to me, I'm sure his own mortality was on his mind. I should have been more aware and understanding of these impacts in his life.

Total Commitment

WE SETTLED in a rental house back in Marietta until we could sell our house in Jackson, and day by day Lou grew more tense and withdrawn. He never talked about his business and rarely about our finances, so I could only imagine that his sales were not materializing. He was traveling, despite the fact that he had not fully recovered from his hip replacements.

It was about that time that my friends Jackie Beavers and Janice Brannon called. They had been researching a direct sales company called NSA that sold water filters and air filters. "We've studied the company and the marketing plan," Jackie said, "and it's the best I've ever seen. We're going to do this and we can't imagine doing it without you."

A night or two later I told Lou that I had talked with Jackie and was considering NSA to help generate some additional income. I didn't explain it the right way, because Lou quickly became defensive, as if I had questioned his ability to support his family. I backed off.

A month or so later, however, he told me, "You have to go back to work. I can't handle these bills on my own."

With no income source at all, I had no way to help. We were

sinking fast and desperately needed income.

I had taught school for ten years, but that had been such a long time ago, and I didn't want to go back. I didn't have anywhere else to go but to Jackie, her son Curt, Janice, and NSA. The company had a presentation at an Atlanta hotel coming up soon. Lou didn't want to go with me, but he didn't want me to go alone either. "Take the Karate Kid [Kevin] with you," he said.

So Kevin, who was fourteen, and I went and watched the man at the front of the room draw the business model on a white board. I had a tape recorder so I could listen again later.

There were so many numbers at the presentation—I didn't even try to understand them all. I'm a visual learner, and I was looking at the diagram of the organization. Okay, I thought, you get three distributors, and each of those gets three, and they get three, and you have thirty-nine people. I'm not listening to numbers, but I'm fascinated by that diagram. This is all about building a team. I can do that!

Kevin and I walked out of that room, and I knew this was going to work. My family was going under financially, and somebody was throwing me a lifeline. We stepped into the elevator, the door closed, and I couldn't hold back my excitement any more.

"Can you believe this?" I said. "This is what we've been looking for. We can do this, Kevin. This will work for us."

Kevin asked, "So does this mean we're going to be rich?"

"I don't think we'll get rich," I said, "but it could get us through this tough time."

Failure was not an option. I had no choice but to passionately believe in what we were doing. Since we had just left Jackson, and we had so many friends back there, it seemed Mississippi was the best place to start building our team.

I rented a room at the Holiday Inn in Jackson and then got on the telephone and invited thirty of our Mississippi friends.

I couldn't wait to see them all again and share my excitement. There was another NSA presentation in Atlanta the night before, and I went back with a tape recorder and sat on the front row to make sure I absorbed it.

The next morning Kevin rode with me to Jackson, and as soon as we got out of our driveway, I started the tape I had made of the sales presentation. Kevin sat there bored as I listened to the marketing plan, and as soon as it ended, I asked him to rewind it and play it again.

"Seriously, Mom?" he said.

"Honey, I need to know all the details so I can answer any questions they ask," I said.

The tape played all the way through, and I asked Kevin to rewind it one more time.

"Please," he said, "not again."

"We have thirty people coming to hear this. We have to get it right."

I listened to that tape for four hundred miles.

We arrived in Jackson, and the Holiday Inn had put a nice sign by the door to the meeting room. My parents were the first to arrive.

"I hope there are enough chairs," I said.

"I'll get more if you need them," Daddy said.

We waited in the hall so I could greet people as they came in. At seven o'clock, nobody else had arrived, and I was a little frustrated. I had hoped to start on time so people wouldn't be out late.

"We'll go on in and sit down," Daddy said.

"Count me out," Kevin said. "I've already heard this five times. I'll be in the lobby."

At seven fifteen, my parents and I were still alone. At seven twenty-five, I was pacing the hallway and Mother was wringing her hands. The reality settled in on me. Nobody was coming. Our future was riding on this presentation. Kevin and I had driven four hundred miles. I had invited our closest Mississippi friends, and nobody was coming. I was devastated, but I tried to look like everything was fine to keep from upsetting my parents. They were doing the same for me.

"Well," I said, "looks like it's just the three of us. I've practiced this in my mind for four hundred miles, so Mother, Daddy, y'all sit down. I'm going to show you the marketing plan."

"Good," Mother said enthusiastically. "Good idea, Harriet. Get up there and show it to us."

They must have been thinking, Poor thing. They were always so supportive of everything I did.

I picked up a marker and started writing on the white board, fighting back tears. I showed them the organization and explained the numbers as best I could.

"Great job, sister," Daddy said. "Wonderful. You can do this!"

But I knew he was just trying to make me feel better. I didn't.

We finished, and they congratulated me again, then I went out to the lobby to pay the bill—a hundred dollars that we couldn't afford. *I cannot believe this is happening*, I thought.

Kevin and I spent that night with my parents, and the next morning we drove back to Atlanta. On the highway from Jackson to Meridian, I was really mad. I thought we had friends in Jackson. I took these people meals when they were sick. Lou coached their sons in football for five years. Now when we needed them, where were they?

By the time we reached Meridian, I thought maybe this business wasn't going to work for me. It certainly wasn't going to work in Jackson. I started crying, and I cried from Tuscaloosa to Birmingham. By that time, my fourteen-year-old son was just about ready to open the door and jump out of the car. "Mama, please—get over it," he kept saying.

"I can't get over it," I cried. "I don't know what else to do!"

This opportunity was our last hope.

Then somewhere around Birmingham, a new thought kicked in.

"You know what?" I said. "Those people just don't know what I know. That's why they didn't come. If they had known, they would have been there."

"Uh-huh," Kevin said.

By the time we got back to Atlanta, I had psyched myself up so much, I said, "I'm going back to Jackson."

"I'm not," Kevin said. "I'm not going back there."

Andrea met us at the front door when we walked in, and Kevin told her, "If she asks you to go to Jackson, don't do it. It's a nightmare!"

I could laugh about it by then. I went straight over to the phone and called the Holiday Inn. "You know the room I booked last night," I said. "I'd like to rebook it. I'm coming back in two weeks."

The manager must have wondered why in the world I would come back. He had walked by the room and seen me in there with my parents and twenty-eight empty chairs. "I'm coming back in two weeks," I said.

Lou had come in by then, and when I hung up he asked how it had gone.

"Nobody came," I said.

"Nobody?" He couldn't believe it.

"Not one."

"Then why are you going back?"

"I can't explain," I said, "but I have to. It's like I've been thrown off a horse. I have to get back on."

I took the list of thirty friends, and Fred Davis was at the top. Fred was a builder, an entrepreneur, and a friend of Lou's. "If you can paint the picture for him," Lou had said, "Fred will get on board."

I called him first, and when Fred answered, I told him with genuine enthusiasm, "Fred, I'm so sorry you missed our meeting last night. The good news is I'm coming back to Jackson. This thing is so big that I'm going to have to come back."

Fred offered a polite apology, and I continued. "Fred, you missed it last night. You don't want to miss it this time."

"Okay," he said. "I'll see you in two weeks."

I worked my way through the entire list the same way, "You missed it last night, but this is really big . . ."

Two weeks later I drove back to the Jackson Holiday Inn, this time by myself, praying every mile for God to be with me. Our survival as a family depended on it.

At the Holiday Inn the same room was set up with the same thirty chairs and the same sign outside the door. A few minutes before seven o'clock, I almost started crying for joy when Fred Davis came down the hallway. Over the next few minutes more than a dozen of our friends arrived. God was answering my prayers. As I picked up the marker to start, I realized that my first presentation with my parents had been a dress rehearsal. This time it was real.

And Lou was right. Fred got it. I don't remember how many from that first night became distributors, but Fred did, and when he built a condominium complex in Destin, Florida, he installed a water filter in every unit.

God had opened a door of opportunity for us, and we were on our way.

We sold the house in Jackson and bought a beautiful home in Marietta that, in hindsight, was too much for us. We sank all our equity into the down payment and still had a considerable monthly mortgage payment. But with my income from NSA growing every month, money no longer was a concern.

Unconditional Love Will Break Through

IN THE YEAR prior to Lou's leaving, our communications were shutting down. Neither of us knew how to develop true intimacy—to speak our deepest desires. We didn't know how to bear our true selves, for fear of rejection. So week by week, we talked less.

"You know, I'm considering leaving after the wedding," he had said back when Christy and Barry were getting married. He might leave me, but at my core I didn't think Lou would ever leave the children.

Then the company he was working for downsized and eliminated his job just as my business was beginning to thrive. I had become a national marketing director, which gave us a benefits package that included health care. Lou didn't celebrate our success.

We needed help. Lou agreed to see a family counselor with me, and when that one didn't work out we saw another. A pattern developed where we would see a counselor several times, and as we neared what looked like a breakthrough, Lou would get frustrated and walk away. Each time the counselor would say, "I don't see any hope of reconciliation," and I began to believe it.

Then we met with Tom Grady, a wonderful counselor, and after Lou angrily left a session, Tom told me, "I can't really offer you hope, but I will say one thing: unconditional love will break through when nothing else will. If you continue to demonstrate God's unconditional love to Lou, that might break through to him."

I told Lou I would like to continue our sessions with Tom, either together or separately, but he said no. By that time he had moved to a separate bedroom.

"We can't keep on like this," I said. "I care about you so much. If you're not going to treat me like your wife, please let me be your friend."

"There's no way you can help me now," he said.

"But we have to do something. I can't live with this kind of tension. We have got to get help or our marriage isn't going to last."

Then after supper one night he suggested we go for a walk. When we got outside, he told me, "You said we need to go for more counseling or our marriage won't last. Well, I've decided separation is the best thing for us."

I couldn't imagine he would actually leave. "But Lou," I pleaded, "Kevin needs you. He's just starting his junior year. Please stay."

He would not. Andrea went away to college and Lou moved out. Just as Kevin was starting his junior year of high school, his father left home. Twenty years earlier Super Lou had been a mentor and role model to high school boys in his Sunday school class. He made such a powerful impact on them that two of the boys later asked Lou to be in their weddings. Now our own son was at that critical age, and Lou had run out of steam.

"I'm going under," he told Andrea, "and I'm taking the whole family with me."

He thought that somehow we would be better off with him out of the picture, and he wouldn't reconsider.

I wasn't sure how our first night would go, with just Kevin and me. Our family had always come together for dinner, and now in the space of a week, Andrea and Lou had left our table. Would Kevin suggest we just forget the dinner table and eat on trays in front of the television like so many other families? Dull the pain by avoiding conversation? How awkward would he be at dinner with just his mother?

I spent all afternoon in the kitchen—my way of coping—and late in the afternoon Kevin came home from football practice. At the last minute I decided to put candles on the table, and I lit them before calling Kevin to dinner.

"Okay, Mom," he said as he sat down. Then he smiled sadly

and said, "I guess it's just you and me now."

In an instant I felt hope rising up in me. Kevin had already frightened me with some bad decisions about school, the people he hung out with, and the things he did with those people. But when he and I sat down at the table that first night, in just a few words he acknowledged the bond that would help us both get through the next ten years. As bad as things would get, as far as he might stray, Kevin would never stop loving. He would never stop demonstrating that love with a hug or a smile or a light touch.

"Yes, but we're going to make it," I said, and for the first time all day I believed it. "We're going to survive."

I continued cooking a full meal every night, and Kevin and I kept the line of communication open. Some nights he would leave the dinner table, and I didn't know where he was or who he was with. But he was home for dinner. We had an appointment.

However, it wasn't long before he did the unthinkable; he quit the football team.

Kevin wasn't big, but he was fast, like his dad. He was playing on special teams, and on the kickoff team he was fast enough to get downfield as soon as the ball arrived and tackle the return man. One time the other team had blockers in a V in front of the return man, and Kevin must have thought he was back in karate, because he jumped high just as they leaned forward to block him. He went over the top of them and landed on the return man.

So when the coach told him at practice one day that he wanted Kevin to play in a junior varsity game with the freshmen and sophomores, he took it as an insult. He thought the coach was just doing whatever it took to win every game—even a JV game. Kevin told him he wouldn't do it, and the argument escalated quickly. Kevin threw down his helmet, stomped off the practice field, and said he was done with football. He was rebelling against all authority, even if it meant giving up a game he really enjoyed.

Lou was crushed, and I was angry with the coach, who knew what Kevin was going through at home. Kevin's teammates supported him in a public way. On Friday, game day, the players always wore their football jerseys to school, but on that first Friday some of them didn't wear their jerseys. It was their silent protest—their way of standing in solidarity with Kevin.

Leaving behind the discipline of football, Kevin started unraveling faster. Instead of hanging out with his teammates, he made friends with more of a party crowd. He was reinventing himself, and he realized people were drawn to him when he was the fun guy who would do anything. He became the life of the party. In time that grew into a self-destructive personality. People thought Kevin was daring and crazy, and he went with it. Nobody messes with the crazy guy, especially if he has a black belt in karate.

✛

Your parents' relationship means everything. As I saw my parents starting to separate, I got really confused. The ground I was standing on started to crumble underneath me. Any security I had was false, and I started to doubt everything. If that's not real, then what is real? Is my relationship with God real? I was questioning everything.

— Kevin

✛

Sometimes my son, who had been filled with tenderness, could be so hard, as if his heart was pumping unforgiveness and bitterness. One night at dinner I said, "Kevin, you act like you don't care anymore."

"I quit caring," he said. "It hurts too much to care."

I knew he didn't really believe that, but it was becoming true for him.

In my prayers I began to recite Ezekiel 36:26 for Kevin, inserting his name into the scripture and praying it as a promise from God:

I remember sitting down to dinner with my parents when they explained that they were separating. They were both in tears. I don't remember if I was crying.

It took a few days for the anger and resentment to set in, but then it started to eat away at me. He waited until Andrea left for college. Didn't he love me enough to wait until I had left?

That was when I put up a shield. Anything goes from here on. It's all about me.

I played it off like I didn't care. But at sixteen, a boy needs a dad. It was a tough time for me to accept that. Instead of dealing with it, I went into complete survival mode. That was the only way I knew to deal with it. I became selfish and self-centered. I sought refuge in whatever pleased me. I surrounded myself with other people who were hurting. We knew how to deal with it. We were a ship of fools. Nobody knew anybody had a problem because everybody had a problem. That felt like the norm.

— Kevin

"I will give Kevin a new heart, and I will put a new spirit in him. I will take out Kevin's stony, stubborn heart and give him a tender, responsive heart."

One night he was out really late, and I was praying for him on my knees at my bedside. I didn't hear him come in until he was standing at my bedroom door. I looked up, and he had such a look of compassion.

He came over and put his arm around me and asked, "Mom, when are you going to understand God isn't hearing us anymore?"

The tears came quickly, and I said, "Honey, that's not true. God is hearing us."

Kevin's tenderness—his unconditional love—in that moment

was a sign that God heard and was answering my prayer. Still, a deep sadness grew in me.

The Beginning of Lou's Journey

LOU MOVED from our house into an apartment nearby, but he wasn't there long before he went back to his grandmother's house in Midtown. His grandmother had died years earlier, and Lou's Aunt Moddie had inherited the big, rambling former boarding-house on Myrtle Street. Aunt Moddie didn't take boarders, as her mother had from the 1930s to the 1950s, but she took in Lou.

Lou and I stayed in touch to varying degrees throughout our separation. When Christy and Barry invited the family to their house for Christmas, they included Lou. He also joined us for several summer vacations.

We avoided talking about the really hard things. We rarely discussed Lou's employment situation. For a time he was selling insurance, then he was a property manager for a real estate company and helping prepare homes for sale. He had other jobs that required physical labor, but as his strength deteriorated because of age and lupus, his opportunities diminished.

He was by no means incapable. His career problem was that as a young man he set out to be a banker, a choice totally unsuited to his strengths.

Super Lou was a coach. He was a mentor. He was a leader of young people, engaging and respected. He was a wonderful father to our three children. Had he turned those strengths into a career as a young man—had he become a high school coach or educator—there would have been no stopping him.

Instead, in his mid-fifties, he was on a lonely journey that took him all the way back to his childhood neighborhood, living with his mother's sister in his grandmother's house.

New Product, Lost Sales

THE ONE positive we had working for us was my business. Jackie had been right about NSA. It was a great company with quality products. I had built a strong team, including a large group of veterinarians who were selling air filters to pet owners, allowing me to become a national marketing director and have family health benefits for the first time in two years.

Then the company introduced Juice Plus and directed its emphasis to the new product. The company president, Jay Martin, is a real visionary with a knack for identifying the right product. When he saw Juice Plus, he knew it was the right product and the right time to introduce it to the market. But the transition was difficult. Many of my distributors left, and within months my income dropped by more than two-thirds.

That was about the time I received the notices from the IRS and the Georgia Department of Revenue that we owed tens of thousands of dollars in back taxes. And Kevin was slipping away, connecting with the wrong crowd at school and staying out late, night after night.

Isolated in the Congregation

MONTHS AFTER Lou left home, near the end of the school year, I was sitting in church on a Sunday morning surrounded by hundreds of people and feeling totally alone. A few of them knew what was happening in my life—that I was a failure. I was too broken and embarrassed to tell anybody.

A woman and her husband were sitting in front of me, and when we stood for a hymn, they shared a hymnal, touching elbows as they sang. Then they sat down, and he put his arm around her shoulder and pulled her closer. She looked up at him and smiled.

That had been the deepest longing of my life, for Lou to be

affectionate with me in that way. Physical touch was one of my love languages, but it was not Lou's way of expressing himself. And now he was gone.

The man kept patting and rubbing his wife's shoulder, and I couldn't stop looking at them and thinking, What does she have that I don't have? Why does that man adore her so?

I could feel tears coming fast, and I had to get out of there. I stood up in the middle of the service and hurried to the aisle, weeping before I reached the door.

The breakdown was coming.

LORD MY HEALER
Jehovah-rapha

God took me to a place where my joy, my peace, my happiness, and my fulfillment no longer depended on Lou. Then He so healed my wounds that I can never be devastated to that degree again. Even if I am, I'm willing, because I'm in a place with Jesus that I did not know before.

1991–2001

Unspoken Prayer . . . Answered

SOMETIMES GOD answers our prayers before we've even prayed them—before we even know to pray them. In the spring of Kevin's junior year in high school, he was making terrible decisions. He needed a stronger hand with summer coming up. Friends in Canada who had been part of our youth group at Eastside Baptist years earlier, had moved there and said he could come up and stay with them for the summer.

Soon after Kevin left, I collapsed at the Juice Plus meeting and was in the hospital and then recovering at home from my breakdown. I'm not sure I could have managed if Kevin had stayed in town. My fear for him when he went out at night would have made any hope of recovery impossible.

God had seen my need and addressed it in advance.

Exchanging My Life for His in Me

BY THE END of my six weeks of quiet recovery, Lou and I declared bankruptcy and the house was foreclosed. Kevin was still in Canada, and when I told him what had happened, his only request was that we find a house to rent, not an apartment. Lou helped me find a rental house in the Wheeler High School district.

I had a lot of rebuilding to do, beginning with my spirit, and I needed a counselor to guide me through the process. The first time I met with Anne Trippe, a Christian counselor, she asked me to tell her my story. When I finished, she said, "Harriet, I'm confident you know Jesus Christ as your Savior, and you want Him to be the Lord of your life. What you're not experiencing is Christ as your life."

Her assessment surprised me, because for the previous twenty years I had been teaching the concept of Christ as your life. I decided to clear up that point right away.

"Actually, Anne," I said, "I was drawn to Galatians 2:20 when I committed my life to Christ, and I memorized it. I studied it and learned its true meaning, and then made it my life verse: 'I have been crucified with Christ; and it is no longer I who live, but Christ lives in me' [NASB]. I teach the concept of Christ living through me to other women. If there's one thing I know, that's it."

Then Anne smiled, maybe a little sadly, and said, "I'm sure you know it in your head, but for whatever reason, you're not

---

Kevin and Lou Connect in Canada

I WAS in Canada the summer Mom went to the hospital, and it was probably the most depressing point in my life. I had no idea what Mom was going through; they didn't tell me. I thought they were trying to fix me. I made everything about me. So I spent the summer in Canada with friends of our family who ran a halfway house up there. Imagine: no family, no friends, and I was homesick for the first time in my life. Dad had gone off on his own thing, and I needed somebody to love on me. I was too cool to admit it, but I needed it and wanted it.

Then Dad showed up in Canada—all the way out in British Columbia to visit me. I needed that visit so badly. We went out camping just like back home, sleeping in a tent by a loud river and waking up the next morning to cook a big breakfast out in the woods.

We hiked for miles one day along a river where the salmon were so thick it looked like you could pull them out with your hands, or maybe walk across the river on them. We followed that river for miles to one of the most remote places in the world.

---

experiencing it in your life."

That hurt, even offended me, and I thought, *This woman is not going to be able to help me. She doesn't know where I'm coming from.* Of course I didn't say that, but my body language may have betrayed my inmost thoughts.

"Thank you so much for your time," I said and left her office, disappointed but knowing there were other counselors.

For the rest of the day, though, I couldn't get her words out of my mind. How could she have so badly misunderstood me. Then the next morning in my quiet time, I began to wonder if maybe she had a point. Wasn't Christ living through me? From childhood I had been compliant, especially with my parents, never wanting

---

Nobody was back there, because nobody would hike so far through the wilderness to get there.

"You hear that?" Dad asked.

"What?"

"Listen. Voices."

They were hard to hear over the rushing river, but they definitely were voices. We climbed up to the top of a little bluff and looked down on a parking lot with cars and people all over. We laughed and laughed. We could have driven to our "remote" spot in the wilderness.

We came back to the house that night and the conversation with our friends turned to our favorite movies. Both Dad and I said we loved Raising Arizona. *We insisted on renting it so we could watch it together, and that night Dad and I were on the floor laughing. Our friends didn't crack a smile. Not even a little chuckle. They just didn't get it.*

Years later Dad and I would remember that night and laugh and ask each other, "What was up with that?"

—Kevin

---

to break the rules or make any waves. Not even a ripple. I was always the one who did exactly what the teacher asked us to do. Wasn't that Christ living through me?

The next morning, again during quiet time, I felt Christ saying to me, "I want you to know Me experientially, not just in your head." It was a frightening realization. Hadn't He been my life? If my lifetime of compliance was not the same as Christ living through me, then what was it? And who was I?

Every morning that week I was hearing confirmation of Anne Trippe's words: "You are not experiencing Christ as your life." I don't know when I have felt more humbled. I called and scheduled another appointment.

"I owe you an apology," I said. "I left our meeting last week really offended because I thought you didn't understand what I was saying. But now I know that you understood very well. So I want you to assume that I've never heard of Galatians 2:20 and teach me what it means to have Christ as my life."

Anne agreed to help me, and for the next year she led me on a journey to freedom, exchanging my life for His life in me, mentally and physically as well as spiritually. I wanted to literally live out the hymn: "Take my hands, and let them move at the impulse of Thy love. Take my feet and let them be swift and beautiful for Thee."

I was no longer going to simply say, "I give my life to You." Rather I would say, "Father, my life belongs to You today. I will trust Your Holy Spirit in me to express the person of Jesus Christ through me."

Of course, living out that commitment is always the challenge. We invite Him in, and then He wants to do something difficult.

Completely Forgiven, Fully Accepted

THE FIRST step in my restoration journey was learning how to forgive, with Christ as my model. Sometimes it was easier to forgive Lou than to forgive myself. And yet it really was hard to truly forgive him. For twenty-five years I had allowed any criticism or sarcastic remark from Lou to wound my spirit. Each cut diminished me further. How could I have failed so miserably as a wife and mother?

Lou came by the house one day, and I was feeling particularly resentful. He said something really sarcastic, and I lost my temper in a way I never had before. I took off my shoe and threw it at him as hard as I could.

"I hate you!" I screamed. "I hate you and what you've done to my life!"

Lou turned and left, and I crumpled on the floor, a victim, blaming Lou, then blaming myself.

I found it difficult to move past blaming myself for the breakup of our family. And what kind of mother was I to have allowed Kevin to become so lost? The desire to rewind the clock and do it all over again haunted me. Maybe this time I could do it right.

Anne helped me see that my desire for a do-over was a destructive mind-set. I had to begin where I was, forgive the hurts from the past, and move forward with a clean slate. Forgiveness, she explained, is a decision—a choice based on an act of my will—not a feeling. The sadness or anger might not go away immediately, but eventually it would if I worked through a process, which involved:

- acknowledging the hurt.
- acknowledging how much that hurt made me feel rejected, unloved, betrayed, and abandoned.
- releasing the person from the debt they owed me. Saying, in effect, "You never have to make it up to me or pay me

back. You are now free, forgiven. I release you."
- accepting the person unconditionally as they are and releasing them of the responsibility to make me feel loved and accepted. I would look to Christ, and no one else, to meet my need for security and significance.
- being willing to be hurt again if God allows it.

I can't count the number of times I've heard the quote, "I owed a debt I could not pay; Jesus paid a debt He did not owe." For most of my life, my performance-based personality convinced me that I had to do something to pay Him back for His sacrifice. That's how the world worked. So I behaved in a way that pleased my parents, my teachers, and my friends. I led Bible studies and worked hard to become a godly wife in a Christian home.

Now Anne was opening my eyes for the first time in my life to the truth of God's forgiveness—that it is absolute grace. I couldn't earn it or pay it back. I could only receive it joyfully. Jesus Christ had willingly taken my sin upon Himself at Calvary, paying my penalty in full.

I began to understand the "exchanged life," that when Jesus became sin on my behalf, I became the righteousness of God in Him (2 Corinthians 5:21). He took my sin upon Himself, and in exchange gave me Himself! The words of 1 Peter 2:24 exploded in my mind: "Christ Himself bore my sins in His body on the cross so that I might die to sin and live to righteousness; for by His wounds I was healed" (NASB, paraphrased).

Understanding and accepting this truth radically changed everything. The Holy Spirit was revealing to me my true identity in Christ, allowing me to see myself as God sees me, His beloved child. I am deeply and unconditionally loved by God, completely forgiven and fully accepted by Him. Finally I could let go of my desire for approval. I could exchange my pride for Christ's humility, my self-centeredness for His servant's heart, my feelings of rejection for His acceptance, my resentment and bitterness for His forgiveness, my control and manipulation for His submission to the will of God.

This would be a moment-by-moment process of allowing Christ to live His life through me. As I yield to Him my mind, I begin to think His thoughts and see my life from His perspective. To the extent that I acknowledge that my tongue belongs to Him, He spreads words of encouragement and wisdom through me. As I open my heart fully to Him, His desires become my own. Christ is able to love others through me, drawing them to Himself.

Every morning when I woke up, I thought, *Sure, I have some issues here I'm dealing with. But the only life I have is Christ in me. He is well able to handle what I'm dealing with today. I'm just going to step out of the picture and let Jesus live this day for me, because He is my life.*

I grew in that year of healing from knowing Jesus as my Savior to understanding that Jesus was my life. I learned to walk in the reality of it, that the only life I have today is the life of Jesus Christ.

That truth set me free from the guilt, free from panic attacks, free from the belief that I had been a failure, and replaced it with calmness. I let go of the outcome and simply let Christ be my life. No more wondering when Lou and Kevin were coming home, if ever. My heart's desire became, Lord, bring Lou and Kevin back to your heart. Make them whole.

I read Dr. Charles Stanley's book *Forgiveness* and allowed it to guide me through the actual process. He suggested a practical exercise that gave me a certain place and time of forgiveness that I could refer to later when old negative feelings returned.

I placed a photograph of Lou in an empty chair and told him what he had done to hurt me and how that made me feel. I didn't hold back the emotions; they were part of the process. Then I told him that I was releasing him from the debt—that I loved and accepted him, and he was no longer responsible for meeting my needs. I had listed the wounds, generally, on a sheet of paper, and to demonstrate the debt was cancelled, I tore the paper up and threw it away.

"Forgiveness," I reminded myself, "is an act of the will done by faith before God in which I give up my right to hold another person accountable for the wrong he has done me."

Set Free!

QUESTIONS STILL came from family and friends who knew our situation: How long is this going on? How long will you be a married woman with no husband? Why don't you file for divorce? These were people who loved and cared for me, and I couldn't simply ignore them. Lou still had made no indication whether he might someday come home or file for divorce. His indecision left me neither married nor single.

I couldn't go further in my restoration without a resolution. If Lou wouldn't decide, then I would have to decide for us. To do that, I needed to hear from God. Setting aside a weekend for prayer, I began on Friday afternoon by praying, "Lord, I cannot go through this uncertainty anymore. Should I take the reins and file for divorce like everyone is telling me? I need to know, and I'll stay here in the house until You let me know. I'm ready to do what You tell me."

I spent Friday evening and Saturday morning in prayer, praise, and the Word, but I did not have an answer. On Saturday afternoon I considered my role in the failure of our marriage. Still in my pajamas, I went to the reclining chair, and I prayed, "Lord, I want to know my part in all of this. Show me what it was like to be married to me. Show me what Lou experienced. I'm ready to listen."

That was a turning point.

What God did for me that day I wouldn't have been ready to receive before then. (Don't ever ask this question if you're not prepared to see the answer. It's not pretty.) In my heart of hearts, until that Saturday afternoon, I felt like the failure of our marriage was Lou's fault. I really think my closest circle of friends would have agreed that Lou was the major offender. It's always both partners, but they would have said it was mostly Lou.

Then God took me back to the day I met Lou, our dating, our engagement, and the early years of marriage. I began to see and remember examples and particular incidents, and I was seeing them from Lou's point of view. I had been treated like a princess as a child, and now I saw a pattern of my self-centeredness as an adult. Lou saw it too. He also saw my judgmental spirit where he was concerned.

With a legal pad and pen, I wrote down everything I saw, and I was horrified. I wrote and wrote, and before it was over, I was out of the chair and flat on my face, weeping over the list. God was showing me my true self—my part in our broken marriage. I had worked so hard to create a perfect family, making sure everybody kept in line with what I thought we should be—and the result was failure.

For three years I had tried to fix our marriage by asking Lou to come back. Like the persistent widow in the parable, I thought if I asked long enough and convincingly enough, Lou would finally see that I was right and come home.

When God showed me my real heart and how I had really looked to Lou, I knew my efforts were hopeless. I couldn't repair Lou or myself or our marriage. Yet God still hadn't answered my question: What am I to do?

I went to bed Saturday night exhausted and discouraged, and on Sunday morning I started again. By three o'clock, still with no answer, I laid the legal pad aside. Despite my vow on Friday afternoon, I had to get out of the house. I took a short walk to clear my head, and when I came back inside I couldn't pick up that pad again. Instead I turned to a Bible study I had been working on.

As I read through scripture, cross-referencing verses, I sensed God speaking to my heart. "Oh my goodness," I said out loud. The answer I had been seeking shone like it was in neon lights.

The Lord made it clear that if I filed for divorce from Lou, He would not love me any less. Our marriage had nothing to do with His love for me. His love was solid. Divorce was an alternative.

"But there is a path, a road less traveled," I felt Him saying, "and there are no guarantees on this road. If you choose to honor the covenant relationship you entered into twenty-seven years ago, I will teach you what it means to be in covenant with Me."

"Oh my goodness," I said again out loud. God was speaking to my heart.

He was not saying to me, "Your marriage will be healed if you take this road." He was saying, "I will be a husband to you, and I will meet your every need and use your life to demonstrate mercy and grace."

I kept writing, faster than ever. And when I had finished, after about twenty minutes, I knew what my choice would be. How could I do anything but stay in covenant and allow God to minister to me? The moment I made that decision, the weight of the world was suddenly lifted off my shoulders. I experienced the truth of the peace that passes all understanding (Philippians 4:7) like never before. That peace swept over and lifted me. In an instant I was transformed from being weary and worn to soaring on wings like an eagle (Isaiah 40:31). The promises from God that I had read and loved all my life were true! They were real!

There was no turning back. I would never again have to ask God what to do about our marriage. I was honoring the covenant. And from that point on, I never referred to my relationship with Lou as marriage. I was in a covenant relationship, and God was going to show me what that meant.

Then I remembered a wonderful illustration of a child who takes a broken toy to his father.

"Can you fix it?" the child asks.

"Yes," the father says, "give it to me."

So the child gives the toy to his father, and while the father is working on it, the child reaches in to help and distracts the father. After the child disrupts the father several more times, the father finally puts the toy down and says, "If you want me to fix this, you're going to have to take your hands off and give it to me."

All these years I had asked God to fix our marriage, yet I wasn't willing to let Him do it without my interference. God was asking now, "Are you willing to take your focus off the marriage and put it on Lou? To let go of the outcome and rest in Me? Then I can teach you how to love this man with My love—so much that you become an intercessor for him."

"Yes, Father," I wrote. "I will do that. I will let You love Lou through me."

I needed to begin by asking Lou to forgive me. On Monday morning I called Gene Schrader, a counselor Lou and I had met together, and told him I needed to say something to Lou, and I wanted to say it in front of Gene in his office. "But I really don't think Lou will come," I added. "He's so tired of my manipulation." Lou had accused me before of trying to manipulate him, and I knew now he was right. But when I called and asked him to meet me at Gene's office, he didn't ask any questions. He just said, "Yes, I'll be there."

Normally I had felt nervous before our meetings with counselors. Lou had intimidated me when he would say, "She's insincere. She just says what you want to hear."

This day, however, I was so calm. It wasn't about me this time. We went in and I got straight to the point, turning my attention to Lou. "God has shown me some things about myself that I have not seen before," I said. "The irony is that you saw them all along. Some of the things you brought to my attention, I honestly did not see, but I see them now."

At this point I could have asked Lou for blanket forgiveness of my failures, but I knew he would see that as being insincere. I had to go down the list with him.

"Remember the time . . ." I began, and I painted the picture. "Remember how judgmental I was when I . . ."

With each incident I described, I asked Lou to forgive me.

"Lou, the bottom line," I said, "is I didn't love you the way God wanted me to. I didn't know how. I would like another opportunity to love you, but whatever your decision, I've decided this weekend to honor the covenant relationship we entered. I would like to be your wife, but you control that. That ball is in your court. I will not pursue the relationship any further. No more pleading with you to come home. The door is open if you decide you want to be in covenant relationship again."

Lou teared up, but I was able to maintain my composure. He did not commit, but I walked out of Gene's office feeling as free as I have ever felt in my life. God had given me freedom to move on with my life even without ending this relationship. He had begun the process of restoring and healing our family.

Going Public

AS GOD HEALED me deep in my soul, I knew I had to go back to Eastside Baptist Church. I had literally fled the church rather than admit publicly that our family had fallen apart.

I slipped into the Wednesday night prayer meeting, found a spot alone, and waited. More than once I was tempted to stay quiet. Maybe wait until next week, or even leave and not come back. But that was Satan talking.

Finally I stood and walked to the front and asked Pastor Harris if I could speak.

"My marriage is in deep trouble," I said. "Lou and I are separated, and we have been now for a couple of years. It was hard for me to come back here tonight, but this is where I belong. This is where our roots are. Christy was nine months old when we joined this church, and now she's grown and married. This is where we grew together spiritually.

"I need you. I need your prayers and your support. God is giving me hope that one day our family will be restored. My bottom-line prayer is that our family would be restored under the lordship of Jesus Christ. Would you pray with me for that?"

Many heads nodded, and Pastor Harris spoke a powerful prayer for our family. Afterward many people in the room came to me with hugs and words of encouragement. This was a hard-core prayer group, and I knew their words were sincere. If they said they would pray for us, I knew they would.

On Sunday morning I went to Eastside, where there was a slip of paper for submitting prayer requests. I wrote one sentence: "Continue to pray that God will unite our family under the lordship of Jesus Christ."

I knew where that request would go—to a prayer room where volunteers prayed around the clock. I had spent many hours in that room, praying for the requests of others. Now they were praying for us.

In the weeks that followed, people continually came to me and said, "I prayed for your family today." I would be leaving church after the service, and someone would remind me, "I'm standing with you."

Week after week, year after year, I took that slip of paper and wrote again, "Continue to pray that God will unite our family under the lordship of Jesus Christ."

After I'd been back at Eastside becoming more visible, they asked me to teach again. That was a huge step. There was no evidence that any change had occurred in my situation, and I was coming out of a period when I didn't have anything to offer. After a time I felt God leading me to do it. In my brokenness, God had given me insights as to what went wrong. Even more important, I could now help others understand the freedom of finding their identity in Christ. That's what I wanted to teach other women, and they gave me that opportunity.

Kevin's Prodigal Journey

KEVIN WAS a high school senior when God brought Brittany into his life. We had a Bible study for teenagers in our home on Sunday nights led by a young staff member from our church, Jimmy Wolfe. Brittany started coming, and she and Kevin became friends.

✣

My second day at a ranch in New Mexico they took me to the desert and put me on a horse that had never been ridden.

"Any advice?" I asked.

"Hang on."

I was breaking wild horses. You would think that experience would get through to me, but every weekend I was finding a party. Then I got into a fight with the owner of the ranch and took off in the middle of the night. He was just another authority figure to get rid of.

—Kevin

✣

Kevin was rebelling against the entire world at that point, yet somewhere he and Brittany found a safe space outside his rebellion.

"She never judged me," he says. "She was strong and independent, beautiful and compassionate, and she genuinely cared about me. She was always there for me, whether we were dating or just friends, putting up with my ways even when she disagreed with my choices. She's the only girl I ever loved."

Kevin would wander for ten years . . . I mean really wander.

He spent one summer on a ranch in New Mexico with my friend Rusty Armstrong and her husband.

When Kevin came home from New Mexico, I asked if he had figured out what he wanted to do. "I've figured out I don't want to be a cowboy," he said.

Next, Kevin and three friends were watching *Deadliest Catch* on TV one night and decided that looked like a great way to make money. So they bought a Volkswagen bus and drove to Seattle to apply for a job on an Alaskan fishing boat. They got the job and then drove to Anchorage, only to find that the fishing boat had left a week earlier.

Told they would have go back to Seattle and apply again if they wanted a job on a different boat, they were dejected and disheartened, but not giving up. They got back in the VW.

Kevin and his friends got jobs on different boats. Kevin went out for a month on a Japanese fishing boat in Russian waters where he was the only English speaker.

"All the other men were professionals, working hard," Kevin says. "If you didn't work hard, they threw a fish at you. I had a quick temper, and it got me in trouble. It was like a prison at sea, and it broke me mentally.

"I felt like Jonah," he says. "Here I was in the belly of this ship in the middle of the Bering Sea, praying to God, 'You've got to get me out of here!'

"It was an eye-opener, and God was saying, 'Don't you get it by now?'

"No, I didn't."

The boats docked at the end of the month, and Kevin and his friends took their pay, ran to the van, and headed back to Atlanta. I asked him if he had learned what he wanted to do, and he said, "I learned I don't want to be a commercial fisherman."

On the drive back to Seattle, we were hungry and broke and broken. We had no food and no money. We pulled off the side of the road in the middle of the night to sleep because we just couldn't drive another mile. We were so exhausted, coming after truly hard living and disappointment that we didn't get a job.

The sun rose over the Canadian landscape in the morning, and I had never seen anything like it. In the dark of night we had parked next to a lake, and now the sun was gleaming and a boat was coming across the lake in our direction. A father and son had been fishing. I got out of the car and walked toward the lakeshore, and the boat kept coming. Finally the father called out, "We caught too many fish. You guys want some?"

Absolutely, we wanted fresh fish cooked by the lake. The scene was almost biblical.

We were so hungry, and those fish made such a difference. God is so faithful to the unfaithful. His love is unconditional. He loves us even when we are running away from Him as fast as we can.

He caught our attention that morning. We couldn't run from Him. From that point on, though we didn't make an instant turn in our behavior, we started praying together.
—Kevin

Another Lost Son

I WAS LOW on gas, driving to an out-of-town business meeting, so I pulled into a service station to fill up. A young man who looked a little like Kevin in his demeanor was walking into the store. I hadn't seen Kevin in weeks, since he left to find a job in Alaska. Now I saw him in my mind, driving somewhere through the Canadian wilderness between Seattle to Anchorage. The boy turned and our eyes met. He was lost—like he had gone into the store to ask for directions, but nobody knew the way.

I filled up my car and went inside to pay. As I opened the door, I looked back at the boy, sitting on the curb, staring out at something . . . or nothing. He looked so broken, I almost called out to him. But tears were coming fast, so I hurried in and went straight to the restroom and cried. I wanted to go out there and just hold that young man. I would say, "I don't know who your mother is, but I would like to pray for you." I didn't do that. Instead, when I came back out, he looked up and I smiled. Then I got back into the car and prayed for him for miles.

Every time I heard of a young man in trouble with drugs and alcohol, I was all over it. "I'll pray for your son," I said. God let me know I was planting seeds of faith for my own son when I prayed for their sons.

Always Connected

AS FAR AWAY as he went, Kevin never truly left the family. And he always stayed connected with Brittany. However, when he arrived back home from Alaska, she had left for college in Colorado. Kevin decided the Rocky Mountains might be a good place to relocate. He drove out to Fort Collins and got a job flipping burgers, then bartending—the last place he needed to be.

I never understood how Kevin could have had such a heart for God and then drifted so far. With his behavior he piled up a lot of garbage in his heart and appeared to have completely buried his love for God. But when we love God the way Kevin had loved Him, there isn't enough garbage in the world to cover it up completely.

Always he was drawn to Brittany. When he found her at Colorado State University, he knew for the first time that he was at risk of losing her forever. At eighteen, she had mapped out a plan and was pursuing it. At twenty-one, he was drifting aimlessly, not even thinking about tomorrow.

Kevin thought she deserved something he was not offering, so he pulled out the Yellow Pages and found the Rocky Mountain College of Art and Design in Denver. Four years later he had his art degree, which he had thought would "fix" him. Instead he was more broken by his addictions than ever, and he began to sabotage his relationship with Brittany. She moved back to Atlanta and Kevin followed, even though they were no longer a couple. He was ready to move closer to home.

Building a Business from the Basement

WHILE KEVIN was in Colorado, I was trying to build some financial footing from Carey and Sheila's basement apartment. You've seen the signs in the windows: CHECKS CASHED HERE. Maybe you've wondered about the financial situations of people who might rely on those services.

Mine was a disaster. My family and friends would not have allowed me to be without a home, but I was close enough to the edge to see how someone could end up in a shelter.

When Lou and I had declared bankruptcy, my credit cards were shut down, and because the Department of Revenue had seized my bank account, they could take every dollar I deposited. So the only way I could manage was to have someone other than my bank cash my paychecks, and then I could pay all my bills with cash or money orders. Cash for almost everything, even plane tickets when I traveled to corporate events twice a year. I explained my predicament to a close friend, who was astonished. "That's impossible," she said. "You have to have a credit card."

She offered to give me one of hers and add my name to her account. I could pay her cash when my paycheck came.

Carey's son-in-law, Scott Merritt, also a CPA, taught me how to balance my checkbook and manage my finances. We met monthly, and no matter how bad things looked or how inadequate I felt, he always offered encouragement. "Harriet," he said, "you've done great. Look what you've accomplished this month." He wasn't patronizing; he was able to find points of real financial progress.

Every month I also stood in line at the post office, carrying enough cash to make me uncomfortable, to buy a money order for the IRS and another one for the Georgia Department of Revenue. I was paying them more than the monthly amount we had negotiated so I could get rid of that debt burden as fast as possible.

In the meantime I was living in Carey and Sheila's basement, which was set up like a small efficiency apartment with a little kitchen. Against one wall I had a bed; against another wall, a sofa; and against the third wall, a desk—my bedroom, my living room, and my office. I had a television, which I rarely turned on, and a telephone, my most important tool. I didn't have a cell phone or a computer or email—just that telephone, and I was calling people day and night, building my business.

"Lord," I prayed, "You gave me the ability to build a team once. I'm going to throw my heart into building a successful business again. I will get up every morning with a strong desire to work hard."

The business grew quickly and checks started growing. I was feeling good again. When you're busy and productive, you don't have time to feel sorry for yourself.

I didn't make sales calls or presentations. Instead I had conversations with friends, catching up with some I hadn't visited with in years. We might get together for coffee, or if they lived out of town, I would ask if I could send them some information about Juice Plus. But I never pressed. We just talked.

"I've found something I believe in so strongly that I want

everybody I care about to be aware of this," I might say, "and I thought about you and your family. If I send a cassette tape in the mail to you, do you think you could listen to it in the car and give me your honest input?"

If they agreed, then I would make an appointment to call back in a few days and ask if they liked what they heard. And while I was technically selling a product, my greatest joy was bringing others on board and building a team—helping people reach their fullest potential. There is a difference between explaining a marketing plan and helping someone cast a vision of what they can become and then make that vision a reality.

I was working with another national marketing director to help her build her business, and she had no idea that my husband had left. I didn't ever talk to her about my personal life. We were going to the same meeting one day, and she asked, "Do you want me to pick you up on the way?"

"No, no!" I said, probably a little too forcefully. "I'll meet you there."

I laughed when I imagined what she would think of me, her mentor, if I told her to come around to the basement door.

It may sound crazy, developing others to their potential while I was financially broke and living in my accountant's basement. But God gave me a real love for people, a desire to see them succeed. Then Juice Plus gave me a platform, even from the basement, to do that. I was as surprised as anybody, but when I recognized the gift, I knew it was from God, and I wanted to use it for His glory.

Living on Oatmeal

THE FIRST few months were the toughest. The first time Kevin came home, I was ashamed to open the door. All I could think to say was, "I'm so sorry I don't have a home for you to come to."

He looked at me with true tenderness and then put his arm around me and said, "Mama, wherever you are is home. This is home."

Later that fall Andrea came back to Atlanta, and she was so sad for me. Christmas decorations were going up all over the place, but I hadn't put up a tree or anything. "I can't believe you're living in this basement and it's Christmas," she said.

"I know, honey," I said. "But it's just for one Christmas."

It would actually be three Christmases.

My brother still wanted me to move to Kentucky, where he could take care of me, but that might have ended any chance of our family coming back together again. God would have to take care of us. I believed He was telling me to stay with the company and stay with my family. He knew it would work out. There were times when I wasn't so sure, and more than once I almost lost hope of my family finding normalcy again.

One night I didn't have any food in my pantry. I was living on oatmeal at least two nights a week (after twenty-five years of dinners with my family every night, food just wasn't a priority when I was living alone). But that week I had gotten wrapped up in my work, and I literally did not have anything to eat, with my next paycheck still three days away. I went upstairs, and it had been a really busy time for Sheila. Though she was one of my dearest friends, and she knew my troubles better than anybody, I still had to work up the courage to admit, "Sheila, I have a real problem."

"What do you need?" she asked.

"Well, I don't get paid until the end of the week, and I'm completely out of groceries. I know how busy you are this week and you have groceries. So what if I cook every night for you and Carey, and we eat together."

"That's a great plan," she said.

"Okay, just show me what you have in the kitchen."

A Letter Home

OF ALL MY family, my father was hurt most by my decision to stay in the marriage. I was still his little girl—his princess. My pain, my financial struggle, my breakdown all became his burdens, only multiplied. He couldn't talk about my situation without crying, and he never could reconcile it. He and Mother did not visit while I was living in the Barnes's basement.

I sat at my little desk in the basement and wrote Daddy a long letter explaining that I completely understood his point of view. "I know you love me more than anybody on the face of the earth, and that you only want what is best for me. But at this point in time I have to follow what I feel God is telling me.

"The safest place for me, Daddy, is the center of God's will, and I know that's where I am. I don't know what the outcome will look like, but I know God is taking care of me."

A few days later I received a letter from my mother. "God has given me this verse in my quiet time," she wrote. "I know you and your future are in God's hands."

Though my father and mother forsake me,
the LORD will receive me.
—Psalm 27:10

I knew what she meant. She and Daddy were not forsaking me, but they were forsaking that part of my life. Yet she wanted me to know that she trusted God to take care of me. Daddy didn't respond to my letter. I don't think he could respond. It hurt him too much.

My Brother's Short Visit

My brother, Richard, called and said he and Dianne were passing through Atlanta and wanted to spend the afternoon with me.

"Wonderful!" I said. I couldn't wait to see them.

They arrived at the back door, and we had coffee and something I had baked. Then after twenty minutes or so, Richard said they needed to get back on the road. Their abrupt departure was confusing, but I didn't say anything.

Years later Dianne asked me, "Do you remember the time we came to visit when you were in the basement?"

"Of course," I said.

"Well, that almost did Richard in," she said.

Understand, my brother is a strong person and not one to get overly emotional.

"We got in the car to leave," Dianne continued, "and about a block away he stopped and put his head on the steering wheel, fighting back the tears. He looked at me and said, 'Dianne, she will never recover from this. She will never recover.'"

"I PRAY EVERY day that man will someday have the courage to divorce you," my father said.

I knew he had felt that way for a long time, so the statement didn't surprise or upset me. "Daddy," I said, "that makes me very sad, because I'm crying out to God to restore my family for His glory. So when you do that, you're praying against the deepest desire of my heart."

He just shook his head. He never did understand it.

A River in the Desert

TO MY FAMILY and others who knew my situation, I looked like I was in a desert place—like I should have felt empty, and I did early on. A year into our separation I was walking in that desert place every day. That's why I had to be on antidepressants before my breakdown. I was aware of my aloneness every moment—unsatisfied and discontent with my life.

But while I was living in that basement, God satisfied my deepest desires in my desert place. He strengthened me and told me, through Isaiah 58:11 (paraphrased):

> *I will satisfy your needs in a sun-scorched land.*
> *I will strengthen your frame.*
> *You will be like a well-watered garden,*
> *   like a spring whose waters never fail.*
> *I will refresh you in ways you will never be able to describe.*

He took me from feeling lonely to comforted and comfortable.

I read a study of the names of God by Kay Arthur, and one of the names is Jehovah Shammah, "God Is Here." He is present with His children. I began to experience Him every morning as Jehovah Shammah, feeling His presence in a real way. The Holy Spirit, our Comforter, brought deep contentment and deep satisfaction.

Sheila and Carey spent a lot of time, especially in summer, at Lake Lanier, where they had a water ski camp. "Aren't you ever afraid or lonely here?" she asked me one day.

"Not really," I said.

For the first years of my separation from Lou, I had often thought, *If I only had a husband*. Alone in the basement I was learning what it meant to be the bride of Christ. He was refreshing me with "rivers of living water" (John 7:38) from my innermost being.

Bright Hope for Tomorrow

SINCE I WAS eight years old I had played the piano almost every day. I even played for our little church in Hollandale when I was in high school. When Lou and I had just married and he was in night school, I didn't sit at home watching television; I played the piano, skipping around the hymnal to avoid playing the same songs every night. But I always played "Great Is Thy Faithfulness." "All I have needed Thy hand hath provided, great is Thy faithfulness, Lord unto me!"

After Lou left, whenever I played and sang, "Morning by morning new mercies I see," I remembered to look for God's special gifts. Thomas Obediah Chisholm wrote those words in 1923 after he had experienced poor health most of his adult life. He had been inspired by Lamentations 3:22–23: "Because of the LORD's great love we are not consumed, for his compassions never fail. They are new every morning; great is your faithfulness." The song, the music, and the verses gave me hope.

Then I moved into the Barnes's basement, and the only furniture I took was two twin beds. I put everything else, including the piano, in storage. For the next three years all my singing was a cappella, and though I can carry a tune, it wasn't the same. I didn't sit down and sing through the hymnal the way I had played through it daily for thirty years.

Andrea graduated from the University of Alabama and was leaving for a three-month mission trip to China two weeks later. During her short stay with me, I did have some news for her. Dr. Gerald Harris, our pastor for five years in Jackson, had been called to Eastside Baptist. He was our pastor again. Years earlier Gerald and Martha Jean's son, Jerry, had a crush on Andrea, who was two years younger (he was a high school senior and she was a sophomore), and Jerry found reasons to hang out at our house a lot. When Lou had his hip replacements, Jerry visited him several times in the hospital. He also helped us by driving Kevin to get a haircut or to a ballgame. Lou and I thought the world of Jerry. Then we moved to Atlanta, and I believe it broke Jerry's heart.

When Andrea returned from her trip to China, Jerry asked her out on a date—nearly a decade after he had fallen for her. It must have been so uncomfortable for him to pick her up and bring her home to the Barnes's basement. If they wanted to watch TV, I was right there in the room too. They never complained, and we often had to laugh at our awkward circumstance.

Our family was changing, and I began to desire a home again. Lying on the bed one afternoon, listening to worship music, I thought about how content I had been in my little space. Like the apostle Paul, I had experienced what it was like to be in need and to have plenty, and the Holy Spirit had taught me to be content in every situation, whether well fed or hungry. Now this season was drawing to a close. My Juice Plus team and my income had grown, and with Carey and Sheila's generosity with the rent-free space, I was about to complete my tax payments to the IRS and the State of Georgia.

After I made the final tax payment, I began to save that extra money for a down payment on a house. Then shortly before Christmas, Jerry and Andrea came to me and said they wanted to get married. Jerry was already like a member of the family; we had watched him grow up, and his father had been our pastor in two churches. But I wondered if they might wait a few more months. If there was a wedding, everybody would be coming to town. It would be so much nicer if I could welcome them into a home. I certainly couldn't invite them to the Barnes's basement.

They were ready to get married right away, and I remembered Lou and I had been engaged for only four months. How could I deny them the same joy?

As much as I had learned to trust God in everything, I was the mother of the bride, and I couldn't release responsibility for my daughter's wedding. I stressed over it for weeks. (Remember,

I'm accustomed to Delta weddings.) When the pastor's son gets married, the whole church turns out, and I couldn't imagine feeding all those people. The wedding would have to be before five o'clock, so we wouldn't have to serve dinner. We could have cake and punch for five hundred, but no more. So many things to worry about.

Then God's grace appeared in so many ways—church members who offered to help, the generosity of Jerry's family, and one extraordinary gift.

Babbie Mason, the amazing gospel singer, was a member of Eastside, and Jerry asked her if she would sing at the wedding.

"What would you like for me to sing?" she asked.

"Would you sing something for my mother-in-law?" Jerry said. "'Great Is Thy Faithfulness'?"

Their wedding day came and the church was packed, and so beautiful. When it came time for the mother of the bride to walk down the aisle, Kevin took my arm. Then Babbie began—and nobody can sing like Babbie Mason: "Great is Thy faithfulness, O God my Father; there is no shadow of turning with Thee . . ."

The whole thing just swept over me, and the words and the music poured through me until the Holy Spirit was carrying me down the aisle. I had trusted Him with the details of my life, and though I was still living in a basement apartment, He was creating and giving my family this incredibly beautiful moment.

I pulled Kevin's arm closer to me and felt his love—and the love of all my family, and the love of my God—while Babbie continued singing. "Strength for today, and bright hope for tomorrow; blessings all mine, with ten thousand beside."

Then "Wedding March" began, and I looked back to see Andrea on Lou's arm. She radiated joy. He smiled and had tears at the corners of his eyes. Lou appeared to be thrilled and also wistful. Despite his difficulty expressing his feelings, he was a true romantic.

Standing at the altar, Dr. Harris asked who gave this woman to be married to this man.

"Her mother and I," Lou said, then he put Andrea's arm into Jerry's.

We were still a family. God was still faithful. And our hope for tomorrow was brighter than ever.

Prayers of My Sons-in-Law

I could write another book about my sons-in-law, Barry and Jerry, but it wouldn't say as much as this one moment. They had both grown up in Jackson and were close friends for most of their lives. At an event when the family was all together, the two of them came to me quietly and said, "Mom, we know you're out there in the world, a working woman with no husband, and you are vulnerable. We want you to know we're praying for you. We've got your back. We believe in what you're doing even if other people don't."

These young men committed to calling each other every Friday morning and praying over the phone for me and our family.

A Side Road in Lou's Journey

LOU FOUGHT one illness after another, and God was giving me tremendous compassion for him. He needed sinus surgery, and someone would have to look after him in his recovery. He came to me with his problem, and I said, "Lou, why don't you come stay with me. I have an extra bed."

He came and stayed for a week, and then he was back on his way.

A Home for Me

AFTER ANDREA'S wedding I started putting money in the bank again, and when I had six thousand dollars, I got on my knees in that basement and prayed, "Father, You said in Your Word that if I delight in You that You will give me the desires of my heart. Lord, my family needs a home."

I told Scott Merritt, who was still advising me in my finances, that I had saved six thousand dollars and was ready to buy a house.

"Harriet, that's wonderful," he said. (Years later he told me he walked from our meeting straight to Carey's office and said sadly, "There's no way she can buy a house. It's only been five years since the bankruptcy. She won't be able to get any credit.")

Then I called Lou, who was still living with his Aunt Moddie. Maybe the time was right for us to come back together. "I have to get out of Sheila's basement," I told him. "Lou, this would be a wonderful time for us to look for a house together."

He didn't say no, but he dragged his feet and never committed. I moved on and called the Realtor who had sold us our first house. Two weeks later I called Lou again and told him that Daisy had shown me several houses.

"I hope you're not looking in Marietta," he said.

"Why not?" I asked. "That's where our roots are. That's where our church is. Andrea and Jerry are there. Why would I look anywhere else?"

"But there's so much pain in Marietta," he said.

We didn't talk about it again until the day Daisy showed me a house on a large lot on Holly Lane. It had three small bedrooms, so I could use one for my office and have one for the grandchildren when they visited. The backyard was a small forest of oak trees—a beautiful setting.

I made an offer, and that night called Lou to tell him. The line went silent, then he finally said, "Okay."

Christy and Andrea told me later that he was upset that I was buying a house. I was moving on.

Daisy introduced me to a banker who listened to my story. I sat nervously as he looked at my financials—where I had been and how far I had come. Finally he looked up and said, "Mrs. Sulcer, you deserve a house, and I'm going to see that you get it."

In that moment I experienced the truth of Psalm 5:12: "Surely, LORD, you bless the righteous; you surround them with your favor as with a shield." God's favor was on my life. I still didn't know how that would look going forward, but He had taken my hand, and we were walking together. I had such peace about the journey, wherever it might lead. And He was giving me a house!

Weeks later, on a Wednesday afternoon, Daisy and I sat in the closing attorney's office, and I signed document after document—my first major financial transaction on my own. We had started late, and it was after six o'clock when we finished, so I drove straight to church for the Wednesday night prayer meeting. The choir would be singing and the congregation would be all together. I needed to thank God and worship Him. He had brought me so far from that hospital bed five years earlier listening over and over to Don Moen singing, "Give thanks with a grateful heart."

My heart was incredibly grateful. In the car, fighting back tears, I talked to Him out loud all the way to church. "I can't believe this is happening," I prayed. "You're giving me a home! I have a home that belongs to me."

I also needed to stand up in front of that Wednesday night group that had been praying for me all these years and tell them what had just happened. I parked the car and hurried across the parking lot, knowing the service had already started, then slipped in the back door. The choir was singing, and I had to stand there for a moment and collect myself to make sure it was real. I had never before heard them sing "Give Thanks with a

Grateful Heart," but now they were. I was stunned as I listened to them sing, "And now let the weak say, 'I am strong.' Let the poor say, 'I am rich, because of what the Lord has done for us.' My mother used to say, "That has God's fingerprints all over it." I was listening to God's love song for me.

"God, who will ever believe what You've done for me?" I said out loud. "I'm just five years out of bankruptcy and a total collapse. It's not possible." Then I started weeping. "And now let the weak say, 'I am strong.' Let the poor say, 'I am rich, because of what the Lord has done for us.'"

A week later, before I had brought the furniture and moved in, Lou came by to see the house. If he was still upset, he didn't show it.

"No curtains?" he asked.

"Not yet," I said.

"Harriet, I don't want you spending a night in this house before you get blinds on the windows," he said, and added that he would take care of it.

I gave him the key and left, and when I came back the next morning, there were blinds in every window. Lou must have stayed up all night hanging them.

A week later, when I had moved in, he came by and gave me a little tool kit.

"A housewarming gift," he said.

It was no profession of love, but his animosity for me was melting. He was becoming more caring and friendly, the way he might be with a sister.

A few weeks later I was standing at the kitchen sink, and Lou walked across the backyard to the tool shed. He hadn't called to say he was coming, and he didn't even come inside. He was just taking care of something for me.

A wave of emotion swept over me, something I had not felt before, and I said out loud, "Lord, I really love that man, whether he ever loves me back or not. And I know it's You."

I was tapping into God's unconditional love. It was no longer about me. It was God's love flowing through me to Lou.

Praying God's Word

AS I BEGAN to focus on seeing my life from God's perspective, one thing became clear: God was for my marriage and my family. He designed and ordained the covenant relationship between a husband and wife to actually reflect the everlasting love and commitment between Christ and the church (the true body of believers).

God has revealed His will to us through His Word. If I could align my prayers with scripture, then I could be confident that I was asking God to accomplish in my marriage and family what He desired to do. I began to see the truth in James 5:16, "The effective, fervent prayer of a righteous man can accomplish much."

My prayers had been fervent; now they would be effective as I searched out the promises of God and prayed them back to Him. I knew God would do what His Word said He would do. God keeps His promises!

Reading scripture became a treasure hunt for me. As I read passages that I wanted to become a reality in our lives, I rewrote them, personalizing each verse with our names. Affirming these verses day after day ignited a flame of hope in my heart that began to burn brighter.

Only God could restore our family, and He would do it in such a way that He would be glorified.

Glimmers of Hope

DURING OUR separation, it seemed that every time I felt discouraged with our seemingly hopeless situation, God gave me a glimmer of hope. One morning I had a business appointment in Sandy Springs and stopped by the post office there to mail a package. Just as I walked in the door, Lou was coming out. Neither of us would have expected to run into the other in that area, since we both lived miles away. The minute he saw me, his eyes lit up and he called my name. The warm look in his eyes and the affection in his voice as we spoke briefly made my heart flutter. I thought, *Oh my goodness, he really cares about me!*

New Year's Day Prayer for Faith

"ANOTHER YEAR has come and gone, and I've not yet received the manifestation of Your promise to me. But my faith is not shaken. I know the time has not yet come, and I will trust You for the outcome."

On the first day of every January, this was my prayer, and every year I believed, This could be the year that Lou and Kevin come home.

Then another year would pass. December 31 came in years seven, eight, and nine.

Temptation crept in: Give up! Discouragement knocked at the door, especially in the days between Christmas and the New Year. We spent Christmas together at Christy and Barry's home—all of us. Kevin came home from his "far country" for a few days. We have home movies of Lou and me sitting side-by-side on the sofa at Christmas with our granddaughters, Brittan and Aiden, crawling all over us, and it looks so right—just like a couple. Those girls were building a bridge between us as we shared our common love for them. In the years that Lou and I were apart, I might have divorced him and married another man who would have taken care of me. But I could never have found another man who was invested in my grandchildren the way Lou was. No other man would have had that bond. Lou adored our grandchildren.

But he didn't adore me, and after Christmas he went his way, I went mine, and Kevin returned to Colorado.

Then the calendar turned, and I prayed for a fresh infusion of faith. "Do you think your marriage is dead?" I felt God asking me in response. "I'm more powerful than death itself. Don't look at that 'dead' marriage and think it cannot be resurrected. I give life to the dead. I call into being that which does not exist."

I turned to the story of Abraham and his wife, Sarah. "Against all hope" Abraham believed God's promise that he would become "the father of many nations." Abraham was already a hundred years old—his body was as good as dead, the Bible says. Sarah was only a few years younger, and "her womb was also dead." Yet Abraham believed God had the power to keep His promise and deliver to them a child.

I wanted that faith.

The best news for me was that God is the creator of my faith. Our faith is actually a gift from Him, not something we can create or find on our own. A story from the gospel of Mark illustrates this point. A man brought his son to Jesus to heal him of convulsions and said to Jesus:

> "If you can do anything, take pity on us and help us."
> "'If you can'?" said Jesus. "Everything is possible for one who believes."
> Immediately the boy's father exclaimed, "I do believe; help me overcome my unbelief!"
> —Mark 9:22–24

Those three verses summed up my story. Like the first verse, for years I had begged God to help me—to take pity on me and our family. Like the second verse, He answered, telling me through scripture that my own faith could make anything possible. See for yourself in these statements from Jesus about the power of our own faith:

> "Take heart, daughter, your faith has healed you" (Matthew 9:22).
>
> "According to your faith let it be done to you" (Matthew 9:29) .
>
> "Truly I tell you, if you have faith as small as a mustard seed, you can say to this mountain, 'Move from here to there,' and it will move. Nothing will be impossible for you" (Matthew 17:20).
>
> "Daughter, your faith has healed you. Go in peace and be freed from your suffering" (Mark 5:34).
>
> "Go, your faith has healed you" (Mark 10:52).
>
> "Your faith has saved you; go in peace" (Luke 7:50).
>
> "Daughter, your faith has healed you. Go in peace" (Luke 8:48).
>
> "If you have faith as small as a mustard seed, you can say to this mulberry tree, 'Be uprooted and planted in the sea,' and it will obey you" (Luke 17:6).
>
> "Rise and go; your faith has made you well" (Luke 17:19).
>
> "Receive your sight; your faith has healed you" (Luke 18:42).

In fact, without the faith of believers, the Bible says Jesus' own power was limited: "And he did not do many miracles there because of their lack of faith" (Matthew 13:58).

Then, just like the father to Jesus, I responded, "I believe, but please help me believe even more!"

I asked for more faith, and He gave it to me. So I asked again, and then I asked for more.

What I was doing in my outward life made no common sense. The people who loved me most and cared about me most said there was no hope for our marriage. They told me to pull the plug on it, start fresh. I couldn't argue with them. I often wondered how I would respond if one of my daughters had been in my position. This marriage was dead. The love Lou and I once had for each other had long since withered and blown away like chaff.

"Lord," I prayed again, "I want the faith of Abraham, to hope against all hope. You are bigger than life, and You can resurrect this marriage. You've told me so through Your Word."

I might not see it happen in my lifetime; the restoration of our family might be for the next generation. But these things were definitely in God's will, and God had stated clearly that whatever we ask for, we already have, if our request is according to His will (1 John 5:14–15). God is for my marriage, and I knew that meant restoration of our marriage was in His will. This statement from Him gave me confidence to press in to God. This was a bedrock truth from God, and I was standing on it. Everything I prayed for was in His will.

I wrote in my journal, "I'm not sure I was ready for Lou to come home this year. God is still working on me to make me the wife Lou deserves when he comes home." I was changing and growing every year—going deeper into my dependency on God—beginning to live out the things I had believed and taught other people.

A Vision of Kevin's Future

DURING THE time when Kevin was really in the far country, God gave me a glimpse at the possible, and I hung on to it with all my might. I was in Nashville on a business trip one weekend, and a colleague invited me to a charismatic church on Sunday morning. A man playing bongo drums in the praise and worship team looked so much like Kevin, it was uncanny. Years earlier Kevin had asked for bongo drums for Christmas, and he worked hard to become a really good player. Watching the young man on stage in Nashville pour himself completely into a solo, I saw tears streaming down his face. He was worshiping Jesus through his music, and when he finished he threw his hands up and shouted, "Jesus!"

After the service I went straight to him and said, "You have so touched my heart. You have given me encouragement. I have a son about your age who is away from home right now, and you remind me of him. He plays the drums like you do, and watching you tonight, I believe someday I will watch him worship Jesus the way you did."

He said, "What is your son's name?"

"Kevin."

Then he grabbed a pen and wrote Kevin in the palm of his hand.

"Ma'am," he said, "I want to pray for Kevin right now." He reached out and put his hands in mine, and he prayed the most powerful prayer I could imagine. This was a boy who couldn't have been more than nineteen years old, and when he prayed, I was weeping. Then he hugged me and said, "Kevin is coming home."

That night I lay in bed praying for Kevin. Then God placed on my heart, "Quit visualizing Kevin the way he is."

For years I had been trying desperately to get Kevin back to the sweet Christian boy he had been. If I could just get him to Andy Stanley, I thought. All the young people respond to him. I did everything in my power to persuade Kevin and even manipulate him. One Mother's Day he was home, and he asked me, "Mom, what would you like for me to give you?"

"Oh, Kevin," I said, "the one thing I would love is for you to go to church with me tomorrow."

Instantly the curtain fell and his countenance went dark. I couldn't have been more obvious in my attempt to control my son, and we both knew it. Everything I did backfired. Every book I sent him, he rejected. Christy sent CDs of contemporary Christian music, and he never opened them. Finally God practically yelled at me, "Just love him! Love him right where he is, the way he is. Let Me have him. Let Me have his life."

So I finally took my hands off, and God led me to begin to wonder what Kevin might look like if he were absolutely head over heels in love with Jesus again. Sometimes I would look at his face and there would be such a hardness in his eyes, it just wasn't him. Then I would lie in bed at night visualizing him with his arms raised like that young man in Nashville, with no hardness or anger or bitterness in his face—just freedom. I would visualize him standing there with his arms raised praising Jesus, and he was free!

A Particular Time and a Place

THE FIRST time I remember the Holy Spirit speaking dramatically to me through scripture, I had no idea what it meant. Kevin was eleven years old and sat beside me in the pew at Sunday night church back in Jackson. Christy and Andrea were singing in the youth choir. Gerald Harris was in the pulpit, and he read 1 John 2:20, "But ye have an unction from the Holy One, and ye know all things" (KJV).

I had no idea what *unction* meant, and yet I felt the Holy Spirit speaking clearly through the Word: "This is for Kevin." This was a foreign experience for me, but I made a note in the margin of my Bible and dated it.

The next morning I looked up *unction* and learned that it meant anointing, a divine appointment. I read the Amplified Bible translation of the verse, which said, "But you have been anointed by [you hold a sacred appointment from, you have been given an unction from] the Holy One, and you all know [the Truth] or you know all things." That's amazing, I thought. There's an anointing on Kevin's life. I hid that belief in my heart, but I began to see it manifested, because Kevin had such a heart for God.

Then at fifteen, he turned away, not just drifting, but accelerating in the wrong direction. He put himself in truly dangerous situations, and I was scared to death what would happen to him.

God often brought me back to this—there was an anointing on Kevin's life. He could run, but he could not outrun that anointing. And as Dr. Harris had read in the scripture so many years earlier, the truth was planted on his heart and would bring him back.

At one of my lowest moments when Kevin had been away from God, the Holy Spirit brought me to this verse again. Unction. Anointing. Divine appointment.

Then the truth hit me like a fresh breeze. In my business I work by appointment. I know what that means: on a certain day at a certain time. God told me when Kevin was eleven years old that He would have a divine appointment with him. For the last seven years I had been filled with anxiety about this because God hadn't fulfilled His promise.

But He had an appointment. There would be a certain day and a certain time, and He had put it on His calendar.

I could relax and wait for the appointment, expectantly.

Prayers of Samaritan's Purse

MY FINANCES remained tight after I bought the house, going from no rent to a monthly mortgage. I was giving at church, but just barely. Then one morning in my quiet time, I read 2 Corinthians 9:10: "Now he who supplies seed to the sower and bread for food will also supply and increase your store of seed and will enlarge the harvest of your righteousness."

The passage jumped off the page. That meant my only responsibility, if I made a commitment, was to sow. God would provide the seed. "Lord, please forgive me," I prayed. "I have not been sowing."

That day I made a commitment to tithe, even though the amount would not be much, and to give beyond a tithe to other ministries. Where the seed came from was no longer my problem. I would sow and rely on God to supply the seed.

I couldn't wait to get my next paycheck and write out a check for my giving.

In addition to my church, the first ministries I gave to were the Billy Graham Evangelistic Association and Samaritan's Purse, in honor of the impact Billy Graham had made on Lou all those years ago at Ponce de Leon Park.

Months later I needed their help. My family and most of my friends were not supporting my commitment to my marriage, and on some days I was so lonely. I had been sowing into these ministries, and now I needed them to sow some seed in me.

I wrote a personal letter to every ministry I had ever given to. "I have a desperate need," I said. "My family and my marriage are broken. My son is away from the Lord. My husband is away from the family, and we've been separated for years. I'm standing for my family. I've been on a journey with you, and now I need your support. Will you stand with me in this and pray with me?"

Some of them sent replies of encouragement, and on most days I was doing okay. Then one day I heard something about Lou that made me believe all was lost. That old enemy, hopelessness, chased me down and had a hand on my shoulder. I couldn't sleep that night as discouragement descended on me like a flood. I began to think, *I'm crazy to think this marriage can ever be put back together. It's time to throw in the towel on this thing.*

The next morning I walked to the mailbox, and there was

a card from Samaritan's Purse with Galatians 6:9 printed on it. I read it in the driveway: "Let us not become weary in doing good, for at the proper time we will reap a harvest if we do not give up."

It was as if they had selected the card just for me. Then I opened it, and there was a handwritten note: "Dear Harriet, We want you to know our staff prayed for you this morning . . ." The note went on with more encouragement and a commitment to pray regularly for me and my family.

The return address was North Carolina, and the postmark was two days earlier—before I had fallen into this depression. The truth could not have been clearer if an airplane had flown over with a streamer behind it: this came from God. The note had come by way of Samaritan's Purse and Franklin Graham, but this was from God. He knew that on that day I would be so close to giving up.

My heart had grown as dark as the Hollywood Bowl, and Billy Graham's family had struck a match for me.

"I'm not giving up," I said, still standing in the driveway, tears coming down my cheeks. "God is in this, His people are standing with me, and He does not want me to give up hope."

Communion with the Lover of My Heart

For your Maker is your husband—
the LORD Almighty is his name.
—Isaiah 54:5

I'M A ROMANTIC at heart. I love romantic movies and quiet restaurants. My mother once told me, "You're in love with the idea of being in love more than the actual boy."

After Lou left home and our love for each other withered, I

was not interested in falling in love with another man. In fact, I prayed that the Lord would protect me from being attracted to anyone else. But I did want to fall in love with Jesus, and without realizing it, a pastor in Nashville, Tennessee, showed me the way.

My friend Betty Lee Faulkner took me to church with her, and the pastor told how his daughter had lost her way. Her story sounded so much like Kevin's, I hung on the pastor's every word. "My wife said it's like our daughter was kidnapped," he said. "We didn't even know her anymore." The idea of a kidnapping stuck in his mind, until the Lord woke him up one night with the words of 1 Peter 1:18–19, "For you know that it was not with perishable things such as silver or gold that you were redeemed . . . but with the precious blood of Christ."

He explained that the Greek word used for *redeemed* actually meant "ransomed." His daughter had been kidnapped by the deceiver, but the ransom had already been paid, not with silver or gold, but with Christ's blood. "We had to present the ransom to the deceiver and demand that he let our daughter go," the pastor said.

He called his elders together and told them, "We're going to take communion every day and demand that the blood of Christ was enough; the enemy must release my daughter."

I was in tears by that point in the story, and I couldn't get it out of my mind the whole drive home. The Lord laid on my heart to take communion every day for thirty days, and tell Satan he could not have my son. The ransom had already been paid, and he had to release Kevin.

The next day I bought Kedem kosher grape juice and matso bread, and the following morning at five o'clock, I knelt at the table with praise music playing and the Bible opened to the story of the crucifixion. Christ's sacrifice became absolutely real to me in that moment, and I began to weep. I broke the bread and said, "Your body was broken so that our broken family might be made whole." Then I held up the cup and said, "This is the ransom. The kidnapper must release Kevin. Please bring my son back to You." God had made it clear Kevin couldn't come back to our family until he had come back to God. He had a lot of pain to work through.

The Lord showed me I had no power through words or manipulation. I had no power to coerce Lou to come home either. Instead He showed me I had the ability to go behind enemy lines. He told me in my quiet time, "Lou is not the enemy. Don't react to him. Don't attack him. Don't be angry with him. Take all that energy and put it on fighting the real enemy. Weapons of our warfare are not man-made but are mighty, through God, pulling down strongholds, casting down imaginations and every high thing that exalts itself against the knowledge of God and bringing into captivity every thought to the obedience to Christ" (see 2 Corinthians 10:5).

I had been trying to drag Lou to counseling and to manipulate him to my will. I even let my hair grow the way Lou liked it, hoping he would see it and want to come home.

The Lord said again, "You're fighting with the wrong weapons."

"What are the right weapons?" I asked.

"The name of Jesus. The blood of Jesus. The cross. The greatest weapon is the atoning death and resurrection of Jesus Christ."

Those weren't weapons to use against Lou, but for him.

I could deliver the ammunition by speaking God's Word.

The next morning I started again at five o'clock, reading a different version of the crucifixion to keep it fresh. Then I repeated, morning by morning, rising early, listening to praise music, praying, sometimes singing, and taking communion. Those became intimate moments at the beginning of every day, and I understood what it meant to love Him with all my heart and all my soul and all my mind and all my strength in a totally new way. I was sharing my first moments, my first thoughts, and my first meal every day with the Person who loved me more than any other.

After thirty days I felt the freedom to commune weekly instead of daily, so I set aside Saturday mornings. In a way, that was even better than daily, because on Saturday I could spend the entire morning with the new love of my life. I awoke every Saturday with a sense of expectancy.

For many years Christianity had been my religion. Everything was changing now, as I was experiencing an intimate relationship with the person of Jesus Christ and the truth of James 4:8: "Come near to God and he will come near to you."

Like the prodigal son's father, Jesus swept me off my feet. I was experiencing a love affair that I never thought was possible. In our culture we have this idea of what we think marriage should look like for women. TV, movies, and romance novels all create expectations that for the most part are unrealistic. If we instead allow God to express His love through us, then we experience the indescribable joy of that love for ourselves.

Long before my business began to grow, when nothing appeared to be working for me, my sister-in-law, Dianne, said to me, "Harriet, I don't know how you do it. You seem so peaceful."

"I am," I said. "I'm filled with joy now."

The irony was that she had the very thing I had wanted most, a loving husband who was absolutely devoted to her.

Sometimes I feel so fortunate that God brought me to a place where everything else was stripped away and I had to turn to Him. I began to meet Him every day, especially at the communion table. I tell people, "Jesus is more real to me than you are sitting right there," because at the depth of my lowest point, I experienced His presence. My Saturday mornings became a date with the lover of my soul, and I wouldn't miss it for anything in the world. It was precious time, and I woke up earlier than usual so I could have more time with Him.

A Jericho Walk

"ARE YOU married?" asked the woman sitting beside me at the conference.

"Yes," I said, "but I'm in an unusual situation. I've been separated from my husband for six years."

"Really?"

"He left us right before our son started his junior year in high school. And now my son has walked away from the Lord."

I had come to a place where I could talk about Lou and Kevin without crying, but this woman looked at me with such concern, I began to feel the sorrow deep in my core.

"I've been praying that God will bring restoration," I said, "and I believe he will. But I don't know if I will see it in my lifetime."

We continued to talk during breaks through the morning, and at one point my new friend asked, "Have you ever thought of a Jericho walk?"

"I don't know what that is," I said.

I had been reading everything I could find about spiritual warfare, searching for a way to cooperate with God in His work on my family, but a Jericho walk was a new concept.

"You know what the story of Jericho was about?" she asked.

"Yes."

"Well, you just follow that model and let God work."

My response was an odd mix of hope and skepticism—hope, because I really believed God wanted to help us, and skepticism, because the whole thing sounded kind of crazy. I mean, walking around my house and shouting like Joshua and the Israelites?

"I'm not sure I can do that," I said. "I don't know if I have the faith to believe."

"Tell you what," she said. "I'll come out and walk around the first day with you. You can take it from there."

With my new friend's encouragement, hope won out, and I

started laying out my plan to spend a week on my Jericho walk. But I didn't tell another person I was going to do it. It was too far out.

The morning of the first day I went through my normal quiet time with scripture. I skipped breakfast, deciding to fast each day until after the walk. If I'm going to do this, I thought, I have to do it right.

My friend arrived, and we prayed together for more than an hour for God to do a mighty work with Lou and Kevin. At noon we went outside and walked around the house in silence. I couldn't say that I felt God's spirit moving, but I remained optimistic.

The next morning I prayed, fasted, and walked alone. I read the story again from the book of Joshua: "Then the LORD said to Joshua, 'See, I have delivered Jericho into your hands'" (6:2). He made that statement before Joshua and the people had even walked around the walled city on the first day, and yet it was in present tense.

"I have delivered." Not "I will deliver."

God had already done it.

"You've already delivered Lou and Kevin, haven't you, Lord?" I prayed. "You've already done it."

Confidence swelled up within me. The very thing I wanted was what God wanted, and He had already accomplished it.

I hurried out the front door and walked around the house in silent assurance.

Days three, four, five, and six passed in similar fashion, and I began to anticipate the final day. "On the seventh day, march around the city seven times, with the priests blowing the trumpets. When you hear them sound a long blast on the trumpets, have the whole army give a loud shout; then the wall of the city will collapse and the army will go up, everyone straight in" (Joshua 6:4–5).

On the sixth night I was so tired I was almost nauseous. I tried to put a little supper together, but I couldn't stir up enough interest. This wasn't going to work. I couldn't believe I had allowed my hope to grow so much through the week while I walked in circles around my house. I sat at the table and wept, all alone.

I needed to talk to somebody who might understand and comfort me, so I called Betty Lee, my friend in Nashville, and told her everything, expecting her to say, "I'm so sorry, Harriet."

Instead she told me I couldn't stop. I had to finish the walk—find a friend to walk with me, to support me. So I called Martie Hunter, and she insisted on coming over early the next morning.

All morning we prayed and played praise music. We took communion and prepared our hearts. Then at noon I said, "Okay, let's walk."

We started in the backyard so we could finish there, and then we walked around the house seven times, just like at Jericho. When we came around the seventh time, we shouted as loud as we could, "Praise God!"

Then we went back inside and continued praying. After about two hours, Martie said, "Harriet, something has happened here. Something in the spirit realm has broken that we can't see. But we will believe God and wait for the manifestation of the promise."

Then she spoke from the prophet Isaiah: "Those that wait will renew their strength. They shall mount up with wings."

I had been so weak that day, if she had not come, I could not have finished the walk.

There is so much about the spiritual realm that we don't understand, but God broke down the walls of anger and resentment and started giving me unconditional love for Lou. Not romantic love and not pity, but deep, deep compassion. I was not trying to rescue him anymore, but loving him for who he was—seeing the good qualities in his life.

THE LORD MY PEACE
Jehovah-shalom

*The peace God gave me in my heart grew into a
miraculous peace in our family that Lou and I had
never experienced. We enjoyed each other's company,
whether we were with our children and grandchildren
or just the two of us. His coming home meant building
a new home on a foundation of God's peace.*

2001–2013

Blood-N-Fire

A DOCTOR called me and said she knew of a woman working at a downtown homeless shelter who had AIDS. She had been a law school student at Emory and had an encounter with the wrong person.

"She's a beautiful woman in bad shape," my friend said, "and she's trying to help everybody she can at the shelter. I'd like to give her a six-month supply of Juice Plus."

"Absolutely," I said. "Where is the shelter?"

He said it was in a warehouse on Martin Luther King Jr. Boulevard near the Capitol. Blood-N-Fire was the name. "David Van-Cronkhite operates it," he said. "Just ask for him."

By that time Kevin had moved back to Atlanta and was working as a graphic designer at an advertising agency, though his lifestyle had not changed much. I didn't feel comfortable going to a homeless mission in a downtown neighborhood that I didn't know, so I asked Kevin to run the errand for me. He picks up the story from there:

> *If you had been looking for the definition of urban decay in Atlanta, the nineteenth-century warehouse my mom sent me to on Martin Luther King Jr. Boulevard would have been a good place to start. The warehouse looked like it had been abandoned twenty years earlier. Gaps between the bricks were filled with soot and dust from decades of trains running on the tracks in back and Marta buses on the road in front. A sign painted on the front of the building above an awning stated in large block letters: THE WAREHOUSE. Then in a red-and-black script that looked like a sign of spiritual warfare: Blood-N-Fire.*

I parked in the crumbling parking lot and looked across the street at the sprawling Capitol Homes housing project. This was not a neighborhood I was familiar with.

I grabbed the boxes of Juice Plus Mom had sent, walked up the concrete steps to the loading dock, and opened the door. My eyes took a minute to adjust. It was dark inside in the middle of the day in what looked to be a large dining hall. Lights hung from the ceiling, but it was a big space and the light didn't penetrate far. Over the next few weeks in this leaky, crumbling warehouse, I would learn about the real Light, and what true grace looks like.

One of the Blood-N-Fire volunteers greeted me with a smile, and when I explained my errand, she called over the volunteer I had come to see, who was so grateful for Mom's gift. She offered to show me around. She was a law student at Emory and was leaving soon for a mission trip to Africa, and she had been volunteering at Blood-N-Fire. She led me through a door to what years ago had been the storage area of the warehouse, and in this space the walls were lined with huge windows. Sunlight poured through onto dozens and dozens of metal cots with thin mattresses. Several blue tarps hung from the ceiling for makeshift walls, offering the barest bit of privacy for some, but the rest of the cots were lined up out in the open. Not many people were in the room, but the stale smell of sweat and the street mingled with the years of this old warehouse.

At night, she said, every cot would be filled. Most of the people staying in the shelter were single, but there were more than a few children staying with their mothers or fathers, who must have been desperate to have brought them to this place.

People came to the warehouse at Blood-N-Fire for food or clothes or a place to sleep, and they found volunteers and staff who wanted to become their friends. The founder, David Van-Cronkhite, and the staff had made a commitment to build relationships with the men and women they were serving. They believed that when you are homeless, you have no relationships. You've run out of people to call.

"Why don't you come back and see?" she asked me. "We worship every night."

I went back that night, and as soon as I opened the car door I heard conga drums inside. I slipped in and the place was jamming. The drum circle at the front of the room banging out the beat, chairs arranged for worship, but people milling around all over. There must have been two hundred, many of them smiling, and most of them tired, looking like they had spent the day sitting on a sidewalk or under a bridge.

I found my way to a seat on the back row of the chairs and watched this warehouse filled with absolute prodigals. Outcasts. Drug addicts. Alcoholics. Younger brothers. The lost and lonely. People who, in the gospels, were the ones most attracted to Jesus. And moving easily among them were people who looked like me—people with clean sheets on plush mattresses in bedrooms of their own to go home to. Some of them were dancing to the drumbeat with the homeless or playing with children who were staying there. They were touching, hugging, loving. The residents and the volunteers looked as comfortable together as next-door neighbors. It was an intense, radical environment.

After a while most of the people came over to the chairs. Some took their place on the floor on their knees, while others lay facedown on the concrete, worshiping God the way I suddenly realized He was meant to be worshiped. The drum circle went quiet, and a man in faded jeans, T-shirt, and biker jacket stepped up. David VanCronkhite. He was big and imposing. Powerful looking, like a retired tight end who never stopped *working out. He preached the Word with power, and he had the crowd with him. He had clearly won these people's hearts before he started preaching.*

Several times along the way he made eye contact with me, like he was calling me out. He was making me uncomfortable. As exciting as this church was, it was still church. I had long ago decided church was not for me.

After the service ended, people were coming up to him to talk, but he looked beyond them to me, standing at the back row trying to avoid eye contact and get myself out of there. He took an angle and intercepted me in the crowd. I thought maybe he would introduce himself or ask about me. No.

"You realize you're the mailman, and you're not delivering the mail," he said.

What the heck did that mean?

"You don't even know me," I said, and I walked out, weaving my way back through the homeless residents of this place filled with love. I got in the car and closed the door, and I knew he was right. I did know the truth, and I wasn't sharing it. Not even with myself.

I knew I would be back.

—Kevin

A New Creation

KEVIN CALLED and said, "Mom I want you to go to Blood-N-Fire with me this Sunday." I couldn't believe it. He hadn't even taken Brittany there yet. He wanted me to go first.

When I walked in, the music was playing, and Kevin was up front, facing the band with his hands raised. I had never seen him that way before. We went to the Baptist church. But Kevin was lifting his hands to God like he was the only person in the room.

Then he turned and saw me, and he winked. It felt like a

dream, but there he was. He was free. All the guilt, all the hurt, all the anger was gone.

God had kept His appointment. Just like that.

✢ ✢ ✢

I did not hit rock bottom, but I got close enough that I could relate. I can honestly say I'm not sure whether I was convicted to come back or my mom and sisters prayed me back. I know the power of intercessory prayer. I was that guy whose friends lowered him through the roof right in front of Jesus to be healed. Scripture doesn't say he asked to be lowered. They just did.

I didn't ask my family to pray for me. They just did.
—Kevin

Coming Home: Not Like in the Movies

IF OUR SEPARATION ever ended, my dream was for it to be like in the movies, with Lou finally waking up to his love for me, and the two of us embracing. That's not the way it happened.

When Lou's Aunt Moddie died, Andrea and Jerry invited him to move in with them and their two children, eighteen-month-old Hudson and newborn Brinley. As with our own children, Lou never hesitated to change a diaper, and he spent much of his time helping Andrea. I dropped by the house one day, and Lou was sitting in the recliner with Brinley in his arms. She was his little princess. But a year later when Andrea was expecting her third child, they were going to need Lou's bedroom for a nursery.

I asked Andrea if she thought her dad might be ready to come home. Lou and I hadn't discussed the possibility for years, but it looked like the best solution.

A day or two later he came by the house, and I was feeling

so much compassion for him. He looked so tired and drawn. He had been living with Andrea and Jerry for almost a year, and I think they all knew that situation wasn't working.

"Can I make you some coffee?" I asked.

"I'd love that," he said.

Then he began telling me some of the things going on in his life, and as he spoke I had the greatest desire to put my arms around him.

"Lou," I said, "why don't you come home?"

He was quiet for the longest time.

"You think so?" he said.

"Yes, it's time."

Again he was quiet for several seconds before he finally said, "Okay, I'll come home."

My first reaction was a moment of panic. Oh my heavens, what have I done? Am I ready for this? What will this even look like? I had lived alone for ten years, and in those years I had grown so close to the Lord, it was like He was living in my house. And it was a small house! Was there room for another? In many ways, Lou was about to become a third wheel. For example, when I bought the house, I had brought my piano home, and I played and sang loudly whenever the notion struck me. I talked out loud to God all the time. My Saturday morning communion time lasted for hours without interruption. I spent hours on the phone many days talking with my Juice Plus team, and I'm not quiet on the phone. I had no idea how to do this with Lou in the house.

Incredibly, in that very moment I felt God saying to me, "Good, because I do."

So I began to pray, "Lord, I need to step out of the picture and let You work on Lou through me. You know this man. You know what his deepest needs are. You know his heart. You're going to have to do it all for me."

Yet I still had expectations of what our marriage would look like—expectations that became disappointments from day one. In the early years of our marriage, I had looked at my brother and his wife. He was so affectionate with her, and still I longed for that affection from Lou. That's the kind of home Richard and I had grown up in, with our father lavishing affection on our mother. I read that women are energized by physical touch and need to be embraced two or three times a day. Lou wasn't hugging me at all.

I hoped that he would at least be able to talk to me about the issues that divided us. I wanted him to come back to Eastside Baptist Church with me and be a couple again. But Lou had not come home out of love for me or a desire to rebuild something we had lost.

Sunday rolled around, and I knew he would not have the energy to go to church in the morning. Lupus took so much out of him, he couldn't leave the house before noon, so I went without him. Maybe he would join me back at church on Sunday evenings. It would be like homecoming for us to walk into the church where so many people had loved us for so long.

But week after week, Lou was glued to the television on Sunday afternoon watching a football game or the final round of a golf tournament. He didn't just watch. He studied and analyzed. Lou was the guy at the Super Bowl party who didn't understand why everybody wasn't actually watching the game. I left the house for church every Sunday evening disappointed and resentful—a terrible state of mind for our marriage and for my worship preparation. One of us had to change.

I reminded him of the promise he made before he moved back. "Honey, if you come home," I had said, "we have to go for counseling, or else we'll just do the same thing all over again."

"I know," he said. "We will."

Six months later we had not attended a single counseling session.

"Honey," I reminded him, "we decided when you came home that we needed a counselor to help us work through our issues."

"I know," he said.

Another six months passed.

"We really need to talk about this," I told Lou.

"I don't want to talk about it anymore," he said.

So that was that. He was not going to counseling, and I thought, *This is crazy. He's been gone for ten years, and he thinks he can walk back in with no counseling and no guidance, knowing what happened the first time?*

Ten years earlier, Lou's decision would have been a betrayal, in my mind, a wound I would have carried around for years. Throughout our marriage I had expected Lou to fulfill me. My glass was half full, and I looked to him to fill it up. But his glass was only half full too. In our decade apart, the Lord had filled my cup until it was running over—and He was still pouring!

I wrote in my prayer journal, "I have no clue how to meet this man's most basic needs. But Lord, You do. If I can step out of the picture and allow You to love him through me, he is going to feel that love. He's going to experience that love."

I was ready now to give up all my expectations of what our marriage would look like. "I don't want to walk through life dissatisfied, wishing things were different," I prayed. "I've been there, and I don't want to go back. I want to embrace who Lou is and to appreciate what we have."

God's response to my heart: "Don't expect Lou to tell you he loves you. Don't expect him to hug you goodnight, at least, not at first. Your love languages may be physical touch and words of affirmation, but you won't get those from Lou. Give up all those expectations."

Then He showed me, "If you're willing to give up those expectations, then I will hug you. I will send you roses and tell you I love you. I will satisfy the deepest longing of your heart in such a way you won't miss it. You won't be longing for expressions of love and acceptance. I am going to lavish them on you.

"But before I can do that, you have to come to me with empty hands. Give up your expectations of what you would have wanted this to look like."

I read Romans 5:5, and saw a picture that changed everything for me:

> *The love of God has been poured out within our hearts*
> *through the Holy Spirit who was given to us (NASB).*

I visualized Niagara Falls and the power of all that water when it flowed. The water (my love) was at the top of the falls. But the falls were dry, and there was no water in the riverbed below. Something at the top was keeping the water from getting through. *Why can't Lou receive my love?* I wondered. *I've done everything in the world to show it to him, but he's still not experiencing my love.*

The dry riverbed below, like so many dry rivers, had all sorts of garbage in it—spare tires, a refrigerator, an abandoned car. That garbage represented the baggage in our marriage, the issues we needed to deal with through counseling. It was so discouraging. We didn't have time to pick up all that garbage. It would take years of counseling to clean it all out, and Lou wasn't even willing to start.

Then the Lord took me back to Romans 5:5. "The love of God has been poured out." It's still pouring and pouring and pouring.

Without water, it might take years for us to pick up the garbage. But what if the dam at the top broke, and this water—not just my love, but God's mighty Niagara River of love—poured forth in a powerful flow? What would happen to the garbage? In an instant it would be gone.

That was the answer. No counseling. No digging back into

the issues that had divided us. God was telling me to let go of all the baggage. Let the dam break. All these issues didn't have to be resolved—just released.

"Okay, Lord," I said, "I'm ready for You to do some supernatural counseling. I'm ready for You to break the dam."

Months after Lou had come home, he still had not hugged me or even touched me on the shoulder. I longed to have him give me a light pat—anything. I hadn't touched him either, because I didn't think he wanted me to. Then I felt the Holy Spirit say, "That's your love language. Express it! You don't have to wait for him to start expressing it. You start!"

That night when I was about to go to bed, I said, "Lou, I want to give you a goodnight hug."

"Okay," he said, though it sounded more like, "Whatever."

Then I hugged him, and I went to bed thinking Romans 5:5, "The love of God has been poured."

Pour on, I thought.

From that night on, if I felt like reaching out to Lou, I did it, and I said quietly, or silently, "5:5."

That was it. Constantly touching him. "5:5."

Years earlier the only counselor who had given our marriage any hope had told me, "If there was hope at all, it will be your unconditional love breaking through."

I did not yet love Lou unconditionally, but God did, and if I could express love, then His love could break through. I felt a freedom in my spirit to reach out whether Lou was ready or not.

A Supernatural Love

THEN CAME perhaps the most dramatic working of the Holy Spirit in our marriage. I prayed that He would give me a love for the things that Lou loved, and before long I began to enjoy golf and football. I didn't learn to love them. I didn't will myself to love them. I just loved them. I sat down with Lou on Sunday afternoon and watched the Falcons play, and I knew almost nothing about the game. I hesitated to interrupt to ask Lou what was happening, but the first time I asked about a play, he explained in a simple way that I could understand. A few minutes later I asked another question, and Lou turned from the game to explain. He seemed to enjoy telling me about the most basic aspects of the game.

With golf we had more of a foundation to build on. Lou and his cousin Ernie had grown up playing Atlanta's public courses, Bobby Jones and Chastain Park. Early in our marriage, Lou and Ernie played in tournaments around the state, usually four-ball and best-ball. Sometimes I went and walked with them, enjoying the beauty of the course. (Lou was so macho at heart, he thought anybody who rode in a golf cart was pathetic. You don't need to be out there if you can't walk and carry your own bag.) The first time I watched a golf tournament on Sunday with him, I relaxed and enjoyed the beauty of the game. I learned the players and their strengths and weaknesses. One night we were at a party, and somehow the conversation turned to golf. One of the men said, "Now, who is that golfer from Fiji?"

I knew right away and said, "Do you mean Vijay Singh? He won again last Sunday."

Lou glanced over at me with a little smile and almost winked.

I was giving my Sunday nights to Lou instead of going to church, knowing the most spiritual thing I could do was to invest my time in my husband—right there on the sofa in front of the television.

Then we took it a step further. Lou watched television at night when I was making calls. If I was going to have more in common with him, I would have to put down the phone and share one of his shows. So I would choose a program we could watch together—except it soon became clear that he would be the one to choose. He chose 24, a popular show based on espionage and a counterterrorist unit, especially agent Jack Bauer, preventing attacks on the United States. There was a lot of violence, but no profanity, and Lou talked about the show all the time. I never loved 24 the way I loved football and golf, but I enjoyed sharing the show with him.

The phone rang one night just as our show was about to start. One of my top national marketing directors was on the line, and she almost never called. She was so independent, it had to be something important. I thought about taping the show and watching a little later. *No*, I thought, *I can't take her call.* "Hi, Wendy," I said. "I watch one show a week with my husband, and it starts in five minutes. Can I call you back in an hour?"

For almost fifty years I had told my husband how important he was to me, but he was not a man of words. That tiny demonstration of my love meant more to him than anything I had ever said.

The next year on the second weekend in April, Masters weekend, I had a business trip to California. It was a terrible time to leave, but it couldn't be helped. I could not miss that meeting. Lou called from home on Sunday afternoon during the final round at Augusta. I was a little surprised that he would stop watching to call. "I just don't want to watch it without you," he said. "It's not the same."

I had prayed for the Spirit to change my heart, and in response, two hearts were changed.

A Wedding, a New House, and Reconciliation

AFTER THREE years together Lou and I were outgrowing my little house on Holly Lane. Andrea and Jerry had three children and another one on the way. Christy and Barry and their two girls had begun a tradition of coming to Atlanta on Christmas Day and staying for the week. And even when it was just the two of us, Lou and I needed more space, because I was on the phone much of the day with Juice Plus distributors. Lou needed a place in the house where he could get away from that.

But it wasn't until we started looking for a new home that I realized the best reason for moving. We were still living in "my house." The children talked about dropping by "Mom's house." Lou didn't need to be living in my house. We should live together in "our house," a place we would choose and own together.

Andrea and Jerry were building a home up in Woodstock, Georgia, so we started looking there. We had seen several houses that didn't suit us, then our Realtor opened the door of a home, and I was immediately drawn to the music room just inside the front door. Lou walked straight through toward the back and called out, "Harriet, look at this—what you've always wanted!"

I looked in his direction, and he was opening the door to a huge screen porch overlooking deep woods. He was right. I had always wanted a screen porch. I was sold. The house was big enough for grandchildren to visit and had an office in the basement for Lou. We started visualizing colors and furniture together.

At the same time, Kevin and Brittany were visualizing a new life together. They were married in a storybook wedding at Barnsley Gardens Resort in north Georgia.

Kevin had mentioned to Lou that he loved bagpipes, and Lou took that idea and ran with it. He found a bagpiper to play "Amazing Grace" as she walked over a hill and down the way toward the wedding party. There was so much grace at that wedding. The weekend was the first time since Lou had come home that we had been together with my mother and my brother's family. Everybody laid aside hard feelings and turned all their attention to Kevin and Brittany.

One of my favorite photographs is of Lou dancing and laughing with six-year-old Brinley, with her long, blonde curls. My family saw how Lou adored his grandchildren, and their hearts had to be touched. Another favorite photo is of my mother, Mimi, eighty-nine years old but looking and acting at least ten years younger, dancing under the stars at the reception with our granddaughter Brittan, who was twelve years old and enchanted by the whole experience.

Lou and I had been back together for three years, and we were feeling like a family again. My only regret was that Daddy had died before Lou came home. I know God could have restored them.

Christmas was coming up, and we had sold the house on Holly Lane. The new house wasn't ready, so Kevin and Brittany volunteered to have us all at their house. Mother told me she didn't think she'd make another trip to Atlanta, especially since she had been there a few months earlier for the wedding. So I put Kevin on the case, and he had a plan. He called his grandmother and told her, "Mimi, we're having Christmas at our house, and I have no idea how to cook a turkey. And, anyway, nobody can cook a turkey like you. Can you come and cook it for us?"

"I'll be there," she said.

So my mother cooked the Christmas turkey, and on Christmas morning God engineered the most wonderful gift. At one point I walked past the kitchen door and glanced in. Mother and Lou were in there alone, and Lou walked over and put his arm around her.

"Mimi, I'm so glad you're here this Christmas," he said. "It really makes a difference."

Then Mother turned and hugged Lou and said, "I'm glad too."

"Oh, God, this is so amazing," I prayed silently. "A stronghold is broken."

It was only a moment, but it changed everything. Lou had been so resentful of my parents for so long. He thought they didn't accept him, and some of that was valid. But when you think like that, you do things and say things that make the situation worse.

With a light touch, a kind word, and a brief hug, decades of hard feelings melted away.

After Christmas Mother and I took a short trip to Helen, Georgia, then we put her on a plane back to Mississippi, and we never saw her again. She died on February 9.

She and a friend had been planning a trip to Belize in ten days, and Mother had gone out and bought a new bathing suit because she was going snorkeling—at eighty-nine! She came home, had an aneurysm, and was gone. She lived a full life up to the very end, and she died with no regrets. Everything that needed to be said had been said.

Can the Kids Come Over?

AT LEAST once a month, somewhere around midweek, Lou would ask, "Can the kids come over this weekend?"

Andrea's four children were barely two years apart in age, and we took them all four at a time—Hudson, Alden, Brinley, and Maleah. We always had the same routine: order pizza; while we waited for the delivery we got everybody in their pjs; then we cleared out the den, made a pallet with quilts from wall to wall, and let them eat right there on the floor. After supper, with lots of pillows piled around them, they curled up and watched a movie we had rented. Granddaddy and I were in our favorite side-by-side recliners, and midway through the movie, we'd bring out the popcorn.

We had to make a more deliberate effort to be involved with Christy's two daughters, because they were in Jackson. Brittan and Aiden were now in high school—Jackson Academy, where our children had been for five years and where Christy had graduated. In spite of his declining health, Lou insisted that we go to Jackson as often as possible to see Brittan cheer or Aiden dance. Brittan also ran track, like her mother had. We made a special trip over to watch her in the finals of the state meet at Mississippi College. Brittan ran the anchor leg of the 400 relay, and when she took the baton and started down that last stretch, Super Lou jumped up like he was going to leap out of the stands and run it with her!

Complete Reconciliation: Kevin and Lou

AFTER TWENTY years, Lou's artificial hips had become so painful, his doctor said they had to be replaced. The contact points where the man-made parts met the God-made parts had become worn, and once-tight connections now allowed movement against the bone.

In those two decades the lupus had taken so much out of him. He was forty-seven-year-old Super Lou when he faced double hip replacements the first time. He was sixty-seven-year-old tired Lou this time. He was tired and growing fearful, having heard that hip replacements the second time around could be even more painful than the first.

I couldn't remember the last time I told Lou how brave he was. He had tried so hard not to let us know what he was enduring with his lupus and his deteriorating hips. As a teenage athlete, he had learned to "suck it up and play with pain." Pain was a sign of weakness, and a "real man" would never let it show.

Fifty years later Lou didn't want to be a burden. He didn't understand, or I had not shown him, that he could never be a burden for the person who loved him most.

The night before his surgery, the lupus tightened its grip—headache, shortness of breath—and escalated to the point that he began to grow panicky about the next morning. I went to him and tried to reassure him, but nothing I said helped. So I called Kevin and asked him to come. We went to Lou's bedside together, and Kevin said, "Mom, give me some time alone with Daddy."

I went upstairs for what seemed like forever and finally went back to check on them. Kevin had gotten in the bed with Lou and was cradling him, talking quietly to him, comforting and encouraging his father. In that moment Lou had become the child, and Kevin had become the father. From out in the hall I couldn't hear the words Kevin was speaking, but it was the most beautiful sight in my life.

All the bitterness Kevin had felt for his father was gone. There was only forgiveness, and forgiveness is the greatest power of all for healing. Forgiveness cancels all the debt, all the disappointments, all the unmet expectations. Forgiveness wipes it all clean and allows you to accept the other person and begin to love them with God's love. Forgiveness frees God to work miracles, and a miracle was working in Kevin and Lou.

Cody

I WAS NOT a dog person. I still have a tendency to be a perfectionist when it comes to a clean house, so we never had an inside dog who ran free all over. But after Lou had his second set of hip replacements, I was traveling, and he was sometimes home alone for several days at a time. He started looking for a dog. When he read about a Greater Swiss Mountain dog on an animal rescue web site, he suggested we call about it.

The people at the shelter brought Cody to our home and interviewed us like we were adopting a child. I think they were worried that Lou, with his lack of mobility, might not be able to take care of Cody. But we convinced them, and Cody stayed.

He bonded with Lou quickly. Cody was a companion dog, extremely loyal. Soon he was following Lou all over the house.

If Lou moved from the sofa to the chair, Cody moved with him. If Lou got up to go to the bathroom, Cody followed him and waited. But mostly Cody lay at Lou's feet when he was on his computer.

Lou and Cody had more in common than companionship. They were both survivors. Cody had a long medical history before he came to live with us: heartworms, inflammation of the lungs, a gastrointestinal infection that required a special diet and medication, and complications from his neutering. He had been living in a kennel for almost a year before we met him. Then he moved in with us, and he didn't have any health problems at all.

Unfinished Business

ON A SUNDAY morning in May, it was like God had thrown open the curtains and raised every window in the house. A cool, spring breeze blew straight out of heaven like the fresh wind of the Holy Spirit, filling the whole world with life.

I was driving home from church, and when I reached our neighborhood street through the golf course, golfers were everywhere. The perfect weather had brought them all out. How I wished I could rush through the front door and call out, "Lou, let's go play a round of golf!"

But when I stepped into the house, the reality of Lou's condition lay like a wake. Lou had sunk so deep into his recliner, he could have been part of the chair. Those golfers were enjoying the sunshine and fresh air—that's what Lou needed.

"Lou, let's get out of here and drive up to the mountains," I suggested. "It's a beautiful afternoon!"

"Okay," he said, but he didn't make a move to get up. In time though, he mustered the strength to get up and change his clothes, and soon we were on our way to the mountains. Along the way we passed familiar sights—the dozens of pink plywood pigs on the hillside at Ellijay promoting a barbecue restaurant, the mountain views from the roadside overlook. I turned off onto a familiar two-lane road toward Vogel State Park, and I thought about the promise we had made to each other more than forty years earlier. Or maybe it was just a dream. We were going to build a mountain cabin, a place up here we could call our own. Lou had fallen in love with these mountains as a teenager, and when he shared his love with me, I fell in love with them too. We had brought our children to these mountains and experienced our happiest times together here.

I pulled off on an even smaller road crowded on both sides by rhododendrons, their flowers hanging like big pink globes. We found a place to park and got out of the car, and the only sound was the breeze high up in the trees.

I felt God saying to me, "Harriet, you didn't keep your promise."

Of course we didn't keep the promise. Look at what had happened to us.

"Yes, look what has happened to you. Your marriage is restored. Your house is paid for. Your children have married beautiful, godly spouses. You have nine wonderful grandchildren. You love My mountains, and you made a promise."

I blurted out, "Oh my heavens, Lou. We haven't done what we said we were going to do."

"What's that?" he asked.

"What we promised! We have some unfinished business up in these mountains."

"Harriet, what are you talking about?"

"Lou, we promised each other we would have a place up in these mountains, and we never did it."

"Well, we've waited too late," he said firmly, as if the matter was closed.

"Oh no, we haven't. It's never too late to fulfill your dreams.

Why couldn't we do it?"

"Look at me, Harriet," Lou said. "Look at me! I'm seventy-one years old. I'm sick. I'm tired. I can't fish in the river anymore. And you're sixty-nine. How can we do it now?"

"We'll go to a lake," I said. "You can fish off the dock. We need to do it now."

"Why now?"

"Well, our children love to be together with us, and with all the grandchildren, we've outgrown the house. We don't have a place where we can all be together. And financially, we can do it."

"You're really serious about this, aren't you?"

"I'm dead serious," I said. "I want to do this. I want to do it quickly. I want to do it now."

"Well, I don't know."

"Yes, let's call the children."

"Well, okay. Call them."

So we drove back home, and we called Andrea. Lou's first words when she answered were, "Your mama has lost her mind. She wants to build a cabin in the mountains."

Andrea said, "Mama, don't talk about this unless you're going to do it. We've had our hopes dashed too many times."

"We're going to do it," I said.

Andrea was quiet for a moment, then she said, "You're really serious, aren't you?"

"Dead serious," I said, and then I could hear Andrea crying on the other end.

We called Christy and Kevin, and we had the whole family on board. Then Lou and I went to bed, and I lay there dreaming of a cabin overflowing with the love of our children and grandchildren and our love for them.

By morning I knew Lou was right about one thing—we couldn't be building a mountain house. We needed to find a home we could buy. We called a Realtor and told him what we were looking for, and within days he was taking us to Chatuge and Blue Ridge lakes in north Georgia. Nothing worked. The houses that were big enough for the whole family were way too expensive, and the ones we could afford would have had us climbing all over each other.

There was one house that I loved on top of a mountain overlooking Lake Nottelly. Lou was less sure. While the view all the way to North Carolina was spectacular, he thought the grandchildren would want to be closer to the water.

"Let's ride up and show it to Kevin and Andrea," I said.

Lou went along, more to be with the children than to see the house again. But when we were almost there, my phone rang. Our Realtor said he had something new to show us. So we backtracked to Blairsville to meet Chad at his office. Standing in the parking lot, I started asking him questions about the house. How many bedrooms did it have? Did it have a nice view of the water? Was the lot level? He was vague with his answers, and finally he said, "Now, Miss Harriet, I don't want you to get upset with me."

I realized there was no house. "You're showing us property without a house, aren't you?" I said.

"Well . . ." he began, and for the first time I was disappointed with him. We had been clear all along.

"Chad," I said, "you know we don't want to build."

"I know," he said. "Just trust me on this one."

So we got back in the car and followed Chad in his truck. Kevin was driving, and Lou sat up front with him. Andrea and I sat in the backseat.

"We're wasting our time," I said, thinking of the house on the mountaintop and wondering if we would ever find the right place.

"No, Mom," Andrea said. "We're in the mountains together."

So many times since she was a little girl, Andrea said just the right word to turn me around, and she had done it again. Lou and I were enjoying a ride through the mountains with two of our grown children on a beautiful summer afternoon. How in the world could I wish for more than that?

Chad left the highway for a narrower paved road, and after a few miles turned off the paved road. Gravel crunched under our tires down a long driveway, then the gravel gave way to dirt. We followed him into a small grove of tall pine trees and shut off the engine. We were surrounded on three sides by water, and even before I opened the door, I thought this could be the place if only it had a house. We opened the doors and stepped out to the quiet sound of wind whispering above us in the pines. We were standing on a point that reached out into the lake. My spine tingled with excitement, but I couldn't say anything. Building was out of the question. Chad explained that the river channel on one side of the point guaranteed deep water all year, and the cove on the other side would be a great place for our grandchildren to swim.

I was so conflicted. Lou had been right—he and I couldn't build a house, not even here. I looked at him, wishing for a glimmer of hope. Lou had built a house for a developer when we were in Mississippi, but that was twenty years and four hip replacements ago. He walked through the trees toward the water as if surveying the land, then back up the gentle slope toward a large clearing, a perfect building site. His expression said, "Maybe . . ."

Maybe! I thought.

"What do you think?" I asked.

"It's beautiful," he said.

Then Andrea said, "This is the place."

"But there's no house," Lou said. The maybe was gone from his face. "I can't build a house."

Kevin stepped in and said, "You don't have to, Dad. This is a family project. We can all do this."

Kevin, Andrea, Christy, Brittany, Jerry, and Barry could take the burden off Lou.

"We'll build it together," Kevin said.

This was really going to happen!

Chad said the lot would be listed for sale on Monday at a below-market price because the family was hoping for a quick sale. If we wanted it, we'd better put in an offer. So we made an offer and bought the lot.

Kevin found a house plan that we all liked, then he began to adapt it to what we wanted. He sketched a fireplace on the outside corner of the wraparound screen porch so we could face the water and a fire at the same time. He showed it to Lou to get his approval, and Lou said, "Kevin, I trust your judgment." I almost cried. We were addressing so much unfinished business, and a house in the mountains was the least of it.

The project gave Lou a goal outside himself to focus on. He and I drove up every week to follow the progress, and Kevin was there even more often, meeting with the builder. Lou and Kevin became like business partners in the project.

God Knocks Down the Walls of Isolation

EVEN WITH the activity of building the lake house, lupus was building a wall around Lou, higher every day. Except for family and a few close friends, he was losing touch with almost everybody he knew. He spent his days at home, and most of the time he was down in the basement at his computer or studying the house plans. At other times he grew grumpier and more demanding.

I took him for his regular visit to the doctor and mentioned that Lou was irritable more often.

"Mrs. Sulcer," Dr. Myerson said, "you would be irritable if you were dealing with what he deals with every day. Have you ever had the flu?"

"Yes," I said.

"Well, the way you feel on the worst day of the flu is the way Lou feels every day. Except that when you have the flu, you know it's temporary. He knows it will never go away. He lives with more pain than most people can tolerate, and that's going to be his life, for the rest of his life."

I hung my head, embarrassed and ashamed. "I'm so sorry, Lou," I said, and I made a commitment right there not to let his complaints upset me. In the car driving home I apologized again and said, "I'm determined not to take your irritability personally."

"Finally," he said, "you get it."

And I did.

After Dr. Myerson set me straight, the cry of my heart became, "Show me, Lord, how to affirm and respect Lou in such a way that he will receive it." I had gone through the first twenty-five years of our marriage believing that Lou's greatest need was the same as mine: to be loved. Now I was learning that his greatest need was to be respected and affirmed.

I prayed that God would also affirm Lou through people outside our family, but with Lou's wall of pain and isolation growing higher every day, I couldn't picture an answer to that one.

Mornings were horrible for him. Waking up with lupus was like being the Tin Man in the woods. He had to be oiled every morning, and the "oil" was his medication. He took powerful pain medication every couple of hours, plus other medicine that directly addressed the illness. Every morning it was vials and vials of medicines, then he sat with his coffee and waited for them to do their work. Sometime around noon he would begin to be able to function.

Two things helped Lou forget his pain: our grandchildren and working with Kevin on the house. Lou went to every possible ballgame or event our grandchildren participated in. At baseball games he always sat behind home plate to offer encouragement to his grandsons and assistance to the umpire. More than once an umpire turned around to tell Lou he didn't need his help, but that never deterred my husband.

The kids were doing a great job keeping Lou up-to-date with technology. For his birthday they gave him an iPod Nano, which he loved, and he bought and downloaded songs left and right. Mostly country music. Johnny Cash was one of his favorites. We were going to one of the grandchildren's ballgames on a Wednesday night when he was downloading another Johnny Cash song, "Guess Things Happen That Way." When Lou played it for me, it sounded like our song for our ten years apart, in a sad kind of way. It was about a man who had left his girl and prayed for strength to make it alone.

We came home from the game that night as tired as if we had played ourselves. I glanced at the caller ID and didn't see any names I recognized. But there were three calls from "Apple."

"Must be some kind of promotion for my iPod," Lou said. We didn't bother listening to the messages.

An hour or so later Lou was watching the late-night news when the phone rang. I went to answer and saw "Apple" on the caller ID.

"Honey, it's Apple again," I said.

"Well, hand me the phone."

I handed it to him and he said, "Hello."

"Is this Louie Sulcer?" the man on the phone asked.

"Yes," Lou said.

"This is Steve Jobs."

Of course, Lou knew it wasn't really Steve Jobs. Lou and Kevin loved to kid each other, and Kevin must have been playing a joke. Lou decided to play along.

"Hey, Steve," he said. "You and Bill Gates hanging out tonight?"

"Louie, this really is Steve Jobs," and something about the way he said it convinced Lou.

"*The* Steve Jobs?" he said.

"The very one."

"Oh my goodness."

Lou fumbled around for words, and Steve Jobs explained that Lou had won the contest.

"What contest?" Lou asked.

"You mean you don't know about the contest?"

He explained that Apple had been running a contest to see who would download the ten billionth song in the history of iTunes. The prize was ten thousand dollars worth of iTunes music. When Lou had clicked *Buy* for "Guess Things Happen That Way," he had become the winner. Then Steve Jobs told Lou that Apple's public relations team would be calling on Thursday. "We'll be setting up a few interviews with the media," he said.

The next day I had an appointment for a manicure and needed to run some errands—nothing important, but I didn't want to be gone too long. I ran out the door without even cleaning the kitchen so I could get back home before any media calls came in.

A little while later I was sitting at the salon with my feet in warm water and the manicurist working on my left hand when my phone rang. It was Lou.

"Harriet, please come home," he said, and he sounded really upset. "You've got to come home right now."

"Honey, what is it?"

"I've been on the phone for an hour," he said. "They're coming to film me for the evening news."

"What do you mean?" I asked.

"I mean Diane Sawyer's team will be here in thirty minutes!" he said. "*ABC World News!*"

The dirty dishes! I never left the house without cleaning up the dishes, and now ABC was coming to my house.

"I'm on my way!" I said.

I jerked my hand from the manicurist and hung up the phone.

"Stop!" I said. "Stop everything. I have to go home!"

"But your other hand," she said.

"I'll come back later, or finish it myself. My husband's going to be on the evening news."

I dried my feet and hurried home, and when I came in, Lou was on the phone with another reporter. I flew upstairs and changed out of my warm-up suit, then ran back down and cleaned up the kitchen in record time. I was putting the last coffee cup away when Lou finished his phone call and the doorbell rang.

I opened the front door, and a white truck with an ABC logo and a satellite dish was parked out front.

"Mrs. Sulcer?" the man said.

"Yes."

"We don't have much time," he said. "We need to interview your husband and feed it to New York in time for *World News*. May we come in?"

"Of course."

And with that, the man came in, followed by another man with a camera and lights. They introduced themselves to Lou and asked him to sit at the kitchen table.

"Mrs. Sulcer," he said, "why don't you stay in the kitchen and look busy."

"Okay."

The phone rang. It was another reporter.

"You'll have to unplug that phone," the man from ABC said. "It can't be ringing while we're taping."

"I can do that," I said, and I disconnected the phone.

They were hooking Lou up with a microphone when the doorbell rang. The man gave me a stern look. I shrugged and went to the door.

"Mrs. Sulcer?" the man at the door said.

"Yes."

"I'm from the *Atlanta Journal-Constitution*. I spoke with Mr. Sulcer on the phone. I'd like to interview him for an article."

"Well, you'll have to wait," I said. "ABC is about to interview him for the evening news."

"Do you mind if I watch?" he asked.

"Come on in."

I went back to the kitchen and looked busy, being careful to keep my unmanicured right hand behind the counter, while they interviewed Lou. He was so calm and composed and funny. It calmed me and made me so proud to watch him.

When the camera crew finished and left, Lou told me more of them were on the way. Fox News parked its truck out front, and then CNN and every local station showed up. I looked out the front window, and our neighbors were huddled on the street, wondering, I'm sure, what in the world had happened at our house.

After two hours of interviews, there were still two crews waiting to talk to Lou, plus *Rolling Stone* magazine had an appointment to talk to him on the phone.

"You're going to have to give us a break," I announced. "Lou has to have something to eat if we're going to finish this tonight. Just give us twenty minutes."

I fixed some soup for Lou, and twenty minutes later CBS was interviewing him for the *Morning Show* with Harry Smith. Then it was CNN. Then one of the local stations.

Finally it was quiet. Sometime around ten o'clock Thursday night they were all gone. We started getting ready for bed, and the phone rang again. A producer from the *Today* show said they would have a car at the house at five o'clock Friday morning to take Lou to a studio downtown for Katie Couric to interview him live from New York.

I told Lou what they wanted. "Tell Katie the only vehicle that can pick me up at five in the morning is an ambulance."

"My husband is not well," I told the producer. "If Katie wants to interview him in the morning, you'll have to send a camera out here."

"No problem."

So we went to bed, and before sunrise Friday morning the doorbell rang. NBC was calling, and soon Lou was downstairs and ready for one more round. In sports they call it "reaching back for a little more." Well, Lou reached back to some hidden reservoir of energy on Friday morning and was as sharp as ever for the *Today* show.

The crew left, and we finally exhaled for good, and for the rest of the morning we watched television. Lou on the CBS *Morning Show*. Lou on CNN. Lou on the local stations. Lou, Lou, Lou.

Then the phone rang.

"Mrs. Sulcer," the woman said, "this is Rosanne Cash. May I speak to Louie?"

"Yes," I said. "Of course."

This time, unlike when all the media people were calling, my hand was shaking when I handed the phone to Lou. "Honey," I said, "it's Rosanne Cash on the phone."

"Really?" he said. "Rosanne Cash?"

"Really."

Lou took the phone.

"Lou," she said, "I saw you on TV. You had no way of knowing this, but today is my dad's seventy-eighth birthday. The fact that you honored him by picking his song and today being his birthday is amazing. You've really honored my dad."

Then she said she and her husband, John Leventhal, wanted to perform the song for Lou.

Lou put his hand on the receiver and told me, "Turn on the speaker."

I turned it on, and Rosanne Cash and her husband played "Guess Things Happen That Way" live for Lou and me sitting in our living room. When they finished, she told Lou that she had never performed the song onstage, even though it was one of her dad's favorites. In honor of Johnny Cash and Lou, she would sing it at her concert in Albany, New York, on Saturday night.

For the rest of the day, and then all weekend, the phone rang constantly. People Lou hadn't heard from in years called to tell him they had seen him on television. High school friends, Georgia Tech friends, even guys from the navy living all over the place called. Everybody wanted to celebrate with Lou.

The next week he went to get a haircut, and his barber wouldn't let him pay. I went to the drugstore to pick up a prescription, and when I said his name, the woman behind me said, "Lou Sulcer? You know Lou Sulcer?"

Our friend David Beavers called from Nashville to tell Lou that he was on page one of *The Tennessean* newspaper. Newspapers and magazines all over picked up the story, from *Fortune* to *The Guardian* in London.

I had prayed for Lou's affirmation, and God had given him something greater than anybody could have asked or imagined. Lou was famous, at least for a while. He reconnected with once-lost friends in those days and continued communicating with them through email, lifting him up when he was feeling his lowest. And he had enough iTunes credits to give his grandchildren every song they would ever want. They usually came to the house to download, adding to Lou's pleasure.

God had knocked down the walls of Lou's isolation in a grand, public way.

Lou's Love Language

EVEN AFTER he had been home for ten years, Lou rarely told me, "I love you." He would sometimes give me expressive cards, especially on our anniversary, my birthday, or Mother's Day, and he would add a thoughtful note. But he still found it hard to speak intimately.

Then all those iTunes downloads gave him a new way to share a tender heart. Every time we drove up to the mountains to check on the progress of the house, he put together a new CD to listen to along the way. We quickly developed a routine: Lou would open the back door and Cody would jump in and stretch out. Then we would get in and I would drive us to McDonald's for a latte, and when we reached the highway Lou would say, "Ready?" Then he would pop in the CD.

Don Williams was one of his favorite country singers, and he was on a lot of Lou's CDs. We were leaving McDonald's one morning when Lou started the music, and out came Don Williams's familiar baritone singing "I Believe in You," a song I remembered hearing years earlier, but had forgotten the words: "It's true," he sang, "I believe in you." I glanced over, and Lou was looking at me in a way that said, "It really is true. I really do believe in you."

For the first twenty-five years of our marriage, in my performance-based acceptance, I had longed to hear Lou's assurance that I was measuring up to his standards. God had now brought me to complete fulfillment in Him so that when Lou affirmed me, he was pouring into a cup that was already running over. It was a sweet, sweet moment. The bitterness and anger had been washed away years earlier, leaving only freedom for God's love to pour through us.

Another trip Lou had put together an entire CD of Scotty McCreery songs. We had fallen in love with Scotty, a wholesome seventeen-year-old baseball player from North Carolina on *American Idol*. We loved his deep, mellow voice, and Lou was thrilled with his country-and-western ballads. We never missed an episode, and each week when the show was over, we grabbed our cell phones and voted for Scotty. "Vote again!" Lou said. "Vote again!" And when Scotty won, we celebrated like he was a member of our family.

The next time we drove up to the mountains, Lou had made a CD he called "The Best of Scotty."

"Ready?" Lou asked as I drove out of McDonald's.

"Ready," I said, smiling and anticipating our new favorite singer. But Lou wasn't smiling. He even looked a little nervous. He pushed in the CD, and immediately I knew why. Scotty started singing, "Maybe I didn't love you quite as often as I could have."

I gripped the steering wheel a little tighter and felt the first tear coming. Lou was apologizing. He had never asked my forgiveness when he came home, and I had never demanded an accounting. God washed away all that baggage with His love and allowed us to bathe together in His forgiveness.

But in Lou's mind, there was still some unfinished business. I looked over and he looked right into my eyes, with his own tear. I had to turn back to the road.

Scotty kept singing, but they were Lou's words. "But you were always on my mind."

I looked over again. This time Lou was staring straight ahead. He couldn't look back. "Tell me that your sweet love hasn't died."

In the silence after the song, I said, "I love you, Lou."

Just before the next song began, I heard, "I love you, Harriet."

Our anniversary was coming up in March, and Lou got tickets for a Don Williams concert in Hiawassee, Georgia. I decided to go all in, so I pulled out my boots and jeans and a western shirt. We drove up early so we could check on the house, which would be finished in June. Before we went inside, we walked out to the point and stood under the pine trees, watching the breeze barely raise a ripple on the water. Then we went inside, and my boots echoed off the plywood subfloors in the empty space. We walked over to the second-floor window overlooking the lake. The hill across the way and the bright blue sky were reflecting in the water. Lou touched my hand and said, "I can't believe we're doing this. How many couples get to realize a lifelong dream?"

"I can't believe it either," I said. "I wish we could stay here tonight."

"Me too," Lou said.

We drove on up to Hiawassee, near several places where we had camped with the children years earlier, and went to the concert. I'm not nearly the Don Williams fan Lou is, but when he sang, "I Believe in You," I looked at Lou, and I cried again.

Another time we pulled out of McDonald's for the mountains, and when Lou started the CD, the first song was the Nitty Gritty Dirt Band singing "Blue Ridge Mountain Girl." It's a sad song about a man who leaves his girl in the mountains for a job in Chicago, "another day, another dollar." All the time he's missing his Blue Ridge Mountain girl, with her green eyes red from crying.

I usually didn't ask if the songs were about me, but this time I did. "Am I your Blue Ridge Mountain girl?"

Lou turned to me and said, "Yes, you are."

I smiled and felt the warmth. *It doesn't get any better than this,* I thought, *driving to the mountains with the man I love beside me and his dog in the back . . . and he's telling me in his own language, "I really do love you."*

Promise Point

WHEN LOU came home in 2000 after ten years away, we had no idea we would have a decade together. He was tired and sick, and he reminded me more than once that he had already outlived his parents. But now we had been back together for ten years. God had restored the years we had lost. Through the prophet Joel, He promised, "I will repay you for the years the locusts have eaten" (2:25). We didn't need literally ten years for that promise to be fulfilled. Lou was home. We were restored. And every year to-gether brought further restoration to our marriage and our family. Then at the ten-year point, we found ourselves stepping into a whole new world with our children, our grandchildren, and each other.

The lake house was finished in May 2010, and we spent Mother's Day there with Kevin and Andrea and their families. Lou gave me a canoe. I had fallen in love with canoeing at summer camp when I was fifteen years old, but my parents never thought it was feasible to have one. Years earlier I had told Lou my sad story, so on our first weekend at the lake he gave me a canoe and a hot-pink life jacket. "I know I can't go out there with you," he said, "but I want to be able to spot you on the lake."

Later in the day, Kevin walked toward the trees down by the lake and said, "We need a fire ring. That's what I remember most growing up in our years camping in the mountains. We always had campfires at night. Let's build a place for campfires here."

Andrea agreed, and for the rest of the afternoon, they, along with Jerry and Brittany and the children, moved stones from the property down to an open spot among the pines until they had a wide ring. Seven weeks later everybody, including Christy and her family from Mississippi, came for a week leading up to the Fourth of July. The first night we were all there, we built a big fire.

To say the moment was "just like old times," when our chil-dren were little and we camped in the woods, understates the joy I was feeling. This was far greater than anything I could have asked or imagined. Nearly five decades earlier Lou and I had committed to each other that we would someday have a cabin in the woods. Never in my wildest dreams did I picture seventeen of us gathered around a campfire outside a brand-new home by the lake.

So I asked everybody to be quiet for a minute, and I told the grandchildren the story their parents had heard countless times through the years—when Lou and I sat by the riverbank up in these mountains and made a commitment to each other to someday have our own place.

"Now," I said, "we should name this place—something meaningful and strong. Let's have a contest. Everybody can submit a name, and we'll vote."

Then Brittan, our first grandchild, said, "Nana, there's no contest. This has to be Promise Point, because you and Granddaddy kept your promise."

"Oh, my heavens," I said. "Why didn't we think of that? Of course."

None of the children knew the deeper meaning of the name Brittan had given us. Lou and I had not told them of keeping our promise to each other or how so many of the promises of God had come true in our lives. Brittan was seven years old when Lou came home, and the other grandchildren were even younger. Their only picture of their grandparents was a loving couple devoted to one another.

Canoe Adventure

PROMISE POINT gave us so many connections with our grandchildren. Lou didn't want me going out alone in the canoe because it was too heavy for me to handle alone. But I could go anywhere I wanted to go with our oldest grandson, Hudson. He gave us a waterproof map so we could explore far from home. Every morning whenever he was at the lake, Hudson would ask, "Nana, are we having an adventure this morning?"

"You bet," I always replied.

One hot afternoon in July we had gone pretty far from the cabin. Hudson said, "Nana, I'm getting hot. I wish we could get in the water."

"Why not?" I asked.

A moment later I learned why not. When Hudson jumped in, the canoe tilted, and I went over the other side.

Hudson was afraid for me, but I was fine, and the water felt nice and cool. I was wearing my pink life jacket and enjoying the float, but after a while I thought Lou might start worrying about us being gone so long.

"I think it's probably time to head back," I said.

Hudson pulled himself into the canoe and held it steady while I tried to get in. But as hard as I pulled, I couldn't lift myself high enough. Hudson tried to help me, but that just tilted the canoe too far over. Then he got out and tried to lift me up, but that didn't work either.

Finally I said, "Hudson, I'm not going to be able to get back into the canoe. It's as simple as that. We need a plan B."

We were in a sparsely populated area of the lake, but in the distance we could see a dock with a ladder. "You get me to that dock," I said, "and I'll climb up on that ladder and get in the canoe."

So off we went, Hudson paddling with all his might, and me hanging on to a red bandana that was tied to the stern.

Every so often he called, "Nana, you back there?"

We made it to the dock, and I got in the canoe. "Hudson," I said, "if you ever tell this story . . ." We both laughed.

Then I thought about how we must have looked. "Somebody in one of these houses looked down from their deck," I said, "and he called out, 'Mildred, look-a there. That boy's got an old woman he's dragging behind his canoe.'"

Becoming a Person of Influence

SINCE MY teenage years I've had a desire to go into full-time ministry. Ten years of teaching school and many more years leading Bible studies had helped prepare me, and after twenty years with the Juice Plus Company, the time felt right.

One morning in my quiet time I was communicating with the Lord through my journaling, and I experienced a huge "aha" moment. "Lord, I can retire now," I wrote. Now that Kevin had come on board, he was capable of leading our growing team, and my residual income would allow me to work full time for the Lord.

I knew God would bless my decision, because it was for Him.

But I was wrong. Instead, almost immediately I felt Him say as clear as day in my heart, "But Harriet, I've already given you a ministry. It's no accident that you are where you are."

The thought astounded me, but then I began to compare the opportunities I might have in full-time ministry with the opportunities I already had.

Juice Plus allowed me a platform occasionally to stand before several thousand people and share my story, and the opportunity to influence hundreds, if not thousands, of people on a regular basis.

How had I not seen the place of influence God had already created for me? "Lord, when did this happen?" I asked. "How did this happen?"

I began my journey with this company because my family was desperate for income. I thought I could build a team, and I loved investing in other people. Then one day a few years later I woke up to the fact that my team had grown so strong, it almost scared me. I didn't know if I was up to the task of leading these people. I wrote in my journal that morning, "Lord, I believe You have placed me in a position of influence, yet I don't feel up to the task of leading this team. But I'm willing to grow and become the leader they need me to be and deserve if You will guide me."

Immediately I began to recognize influencers all around me. My friend David Beavers, who has been with the company since 1988, said, "Our business model is in reality a personal development course cleverly disguised as a business." We are constantly investing in our own development. I asked other leaders what they were reading, and I began to fill my library with books by John Maxwell, Ken Blanchard, Andy Stanley, and others.

To be a person of influence, I learned, I should live a life that others want to follow. You can work up an amazing sales presentation, but more people will lock arms with you if your life attracts people to the business.

The same philosophy works in lifestyle evangelism. Let your heart attract people to Christ. God has given me an opportunity to do that through my business. I see people come to Christ on a regular basis, and then I see them grow spiritually. I find people with the desire to become a person of influence, then I am privileged with the opportunity to help them. I spend more time reminding them how to be a person of integrity and influence than I do teaching people the mechanics of the business.

You can build a business and ruin a life. Or you can build a life. Each life becomes a model. "Look at what a mess we made of our marriage for so long," I say, "and look what happened when we allowed God to repair it. He restored our marriage miraculously when we gave it to Him."

Dr. Gerald Harris, our pastor for years and now our daughter's father-in-law, is editor of the *Christian Index* magazine of the Georgia Baptist Convention. We were at a ballgame with our grandchildren, and he asked, "Harriet, are you thinking about retiring?"

"Oh, Gerald," I said, "I'm more excited about what I'm doing today than I've ever been. I've had a total paradigm shift about what I do. I've been given an incredible opportunity to help build people, and I'm going to grab hold of that. I get to see people learn from their own life lessons and develop into everything God created them to be, then I watch them pass on those lessons and raise new leaders."

The Influence of a Father

AT LOU'S FIFTIETH high school class reunion, he and his friends reenacted the photo they had taken after their Easter weekend camping trip in 1956, with boat paddles, pickup truck, and all. Only one of the fourteen was missing, Lou's cousin Ernie, who had died at forty-two. These friends had stuck by each other for half a century. The other wives and I enjoyed watching them stage the photo, getting a glimpse of the love these men still shared.

They were all Buckhead Boys. In the early 1970s, inspired by James Dickey's poem "Looking for the Buckhead Boys," the friends began meeting on the first Monday in December as a reunion of sorts. These were the men Lou had played football and baseball and basketball with in high school. They had stood at each other's weddings and would later speak at their classmates' funerals.

On the first Monday in December 2012, Lou asked Kevin to drive him to the Buckhead Boys get-together. It would be his last. He had nominated his friend Charlie Breithaupt as Buckhead Boy of the Year, and Charlie had won. Lou wanted to be there when he received it, to share the moment with him.

Charlie had been the organizer of that Easter weekend camping trip. Lou told Kevin the story as they drove into town. Then he talked about the influence Charlie had in the lives of hundreds of young people as a coach and educator at Westminster School in Atlanta and later at Rabun Gap-Nacoochee School in their beloved north Georgia mountains. Charlie's influence in the lives of those young people had been the inspiration for Lou to nominate him.

When they arrived at the event, Kevin knew he might meet some of Atlanta's most influential business leaders. He didn't anticipate the reception his father would receive. At the end of the night, Kevin brought Lou home, and he couldn't stop talking about the men bragging on his father. "It was like Daddy was the guest of honor," he said. "There was a group crowded around him telling stories all night." They had shared glory days together, and Lou's teammates went out of their way to tell Kevin how fast and strong and tough Lou had been. A night like that has a powerful influence on a son, even an adult son.

Lou's influence on our children becomes clearer to me every year. Throughout their childhood Lou was a coach and an encourager to each of them. Like him, they all were athletes as children and teenagers and continue to live a healthy lifestyle. Kevin took that commitment to a higher plane, training for and completing a full Ironman triathlon. That's 2.4 miles swimming, followed by a 112-mile bicycle race, and finishing with a marathon, running 26.2 miles. It was an amazing accomplishment.

By that time Kevin had built his own graphic design firm, which he humbly called Prodigal Design. Then he realized the possibilities of Juice Plus, which had been part of his daily nutrition all his adult life—both the impact on his training and the opportunity to share. He had been telling his friends in fitness about Juice Plus for years. Why not join my team?

Kevin grew quickly in the business. He was a natural. When he was fourteen years old, he had gone with Curt Beavers to install an NSA water filter I had sold. Curt, who was my good friend Jackie's son, was ten years older than Kevin and was like a son to me. In my early years with NSA, he helped me understand the financial side of the business and became in important influence in our lives.

When Kevin joined my team, Curt's influence was crucial to his success. Kevin had watched me build my business with phone calls, conversations, and home meetings. Those tools could work for him, but they weren't his strongest assets.

Then Curt told him, "Find what you're passionate about and go do it. If you surround yourself with like-minded people, the conversations will be easy." For Curt, the passion was golf. Kevin's passion was in the gym, on the road with runs and rides, and in the pool. In that fitness arena, conversations came easy without Kevin appearing to push too hard. He was comfortable with what he was doing and saying. Best of all, the people he was with were committed to healthy lifestyles. Juice Plus became a natural part of the conversation.

Kevin attracted leaders to his business and then coached and inspired them to a level of success that allowed him to sell Prodigal Design and devote himself full time to Juice Plus.

It was amazing to watch Lou take an interest in Kevin's work. Lou had watched me build the business, but much of my growth had occurred when we were apart. As Kevin hit milestones in his growth, Lou followed his progress the way he would follow a sports team, asking about his statistics every time they talked, then encouraging him to grow higher and stronger.

A Grandfather's Powerful Influence

LOU WAS FEELING better and thought he might take up photography, so he bought a nice camera and started learning how to use it. Then Brinley's thirteenth birthday was coming up, and she had also been taking pictures.

"You know," Lou told me, "I think I'll give that camera to Brinley."

"Are you sure, Lou?" I said. "That's a really expensive camera."

"Yes," he replied, "I'm sure. Brinley has talent. She should be the photographer in the family. And she needs a nice case and another lens for it. Let's go to the store." (Brinley took the cover photo for this book with the camera Lou gave her.)

Lou poured so much of himself into our grandchildren, especially at the lake, but also when they stayed at our house in Woodstock.

When Hudson was six years old, Lou started playing baseball

with him in the backyard, coaching him and encouraging him. Ten years later Lou knew he was in his final days, and Hudson was trying out for the varsity baseball team. Lou was concerned Hudson didn't have the right bat, so he had me drive him to the sporting goods store, where he spent more than an hour with the salesman picking out just the right bat. This was just days before he went into hospice. (Hudson made the team.)

Lou was sweet Maleah's spelling bee coach, making flash cards and working with her for hours, and arriving for the event early so he could sit on the front row and encourage her.

More than the gifts, when his grandchildren think of Lou, they remember the time he spent with them watching sports on television, teaching them how to fish, or just listening. My brother, Richard, who had agreed with our parents years earlier that I needed to divorce Lou, visited us often after we came back together and saw Lou's love for our grandchildren. Sitting on the screen porch one morning, drinking coffee, Richard said, "Harriet, I was wrong. I do believe this is Lou's finest hour. He's absolutely the best grandfather I've ever seen."

Alden was the grandchild who sought his grandfather out, then sat with Lou for hours at a time. After two or three fishing stories, the other grandchildren were ready to move on. Not Alden. Alden was a listener, and he quietly captured Lou's heart. Lou also told us often that Alden, with his love of the outdoors, athletic skills, and blond hair, reminded him of himself as a boy.

One thing had bothered Lou for a time: Kevin was his only son, and if he and Brittany didn't have a boy, then his line of the Sulcer name would not continue. More important, he hoped Kevin would one day share the joy of a father with a son. We were driving home from a hospital visit when Kevin called to tell Lou that not only was Brittany expecting a boy, she was expecting twin boys—double the fun.

Kevin and Brittany's daughter, Addison, stayed at our house a lot when her twin brothers were born. Addison reminded Lou so much of Kevin's sister that he called her Little Christy.

One of the greatest gifts God gave us was the opportunity for Lou to know all his grandchildren and to see all of his children as parents. I think we sometimes forgot what an incredible father Lou had been and the influence he had on his own children.

Going Fishing

THE DOCTOR had been so kind. "Mr. Sulcer, I'm so sorry this is happening to you," he had said. "There is no cure, but there are some things we can do."

Lou wanted the truth right up front. "I'm going to fight for as long as it makes sense," he said.

"The tumor in your brain is growing," the doctor explained, "and it will continue to grow. You probably have just a few months to live. In time you could lose your ability to talk. You may not recognize your wife or your children, and then you could lose your ability to think altogether."

He told us of the choices. With surgery, he could reach the tumor and remove it.

"Does that solve the problem?" I asked.

"No ma'am, it doesn't."

"What does it do?"

"It buys you time."

"Recovering from brain surgery?"

"Yes ma'am."

Lou had been so quiet. I had wanted to tell him, "I'm not listening to this. Are you?" Lou had already undergone major lung surgery eight months earlier, two gamma knife treatments for brain tumors, and radiation for a tumor on his sinus. Recovery from each of those events had been painfully miserable for Lou. But it was his life we were talking about.

We left the hospital, and coming out of the parking deck into the daylight, Lou said sarcastically, "Buys me time. What would the quality of life be? Not good."

"Is that what you want?" I asked.

"No," he said. "Not without any quality of life."

"Honey, I will do anything. We can go back. What do you want to do?"

"I want to go fishing," he said.

"Okay, but we'll have to tell the doctor."

"I'll tell him this is the last time," Lou said. "I'm not coming back. That will be the last time he'll see me. From this point on, we're done."

When Lou said he wanted to go fishing, he meant in his bass boat—the boat he had been saving money for since we had built the lake house. I asked if he wanted to go see the dealer. "Not today," he said.

The subject of the bass boat came up several more times, and Lou always hesitated. Finally in June he said, "Harriet, I'm not going to be able to use a bass boat. I want to buy a pontoon boat for the family that everybody can enjoy. And I want it before the Fourth of July when the kids come to the lake."

"What a wonderful idea, Lou," I said.

"I'm going to ask Kevin to look for one for us."

I later overheard Lou talking to Kevin on the phone. "Do it right away," he told him. "Find one now."

A few days later Kevin had found a boat and wanted us to see it with him. It was perfect. Big enough for all eighteen of us, and it even had a grill. On Independence Day we were all on the lake in Lou's pontoon—two grandparents, six parents, ten grandchildren (including Brittan's fiancée, Adam), and Lou's dog.

This was the quality of life Lou and I had dreamed of. That full week we spent at the lake (we had planned everyone's vacations around that time for months) was such a gift from God—

the last time our family was all together. For almost twenty years our family had spent a week together in the summer, and this would be our last with Lou. The pontoon boat allowed us all to go out and find a quiet cove (quiet until eighteen of us showed up) way down the lake where the water was deep and cold and the mountains rose up around us. We anchored and then swam and cooked hot dogs over the grill, then cruised slowly down the lake and watched the sunset. Lou sat quietly smiling and taking it all in—his final gift to the family. Back at the house we built a campfire and sat for several hours around the fire ring talking and laughing.

We were driving back home from the lake, and Lou said, "You know, we put our children through ten hard years, didn't we? But you know what, these last years we've had together have been so wonderful. This is what they'll remember."

"You know that old saying," I said, "all's well that ends well."

"Yeah," he said, smiling, "and we are ending really well."

Precious Days

WE MADE more trips to the lake, even as friends were asking, "Are you really taking him up there by yourself? What if you have an emergency?"

But I was at peace. If something happened, we would deal with it.

Our most precious times were those three years we had the lake house, surrounded by children and grandchildren, or when we were alone on the porch, listening to country music and watching the afterglow of sunsets. For an hour after the sun went down, the water reflected pink, then deep rose, and finally black in the deepening twilight.

We went up in August, and Andrea came with her children. We spent a quiet day together, and I had a feeling it might be our last trip. Lou could barely walk up the steps.

Early Friday morning Lou took a bad fall and couldn't get up. I was so grateful for Hudson, who was sixteen. He helped Lou up, and we got him to the car and drove to the emergency room, where they said Lou had broken his hand. That was the beginning. Two weeks later Lou collapsed at home, and after two exhausting days in the hospital, the oncologist told us they couldn't do any more for him.

"Mrs. Sulcer," the doctor asked gently, "are you ready for hospice?"

I wasn't. That was the first time the doctor had used the word *hospice*, and I had to stop to consider its meaning for a moment. The final count had begun, and there was nothing we could do to stop it. The doctor said, "We may be looking at days here, possibly another week."

The hospital wanted to move him that afternoon, so they introduced me to a hospice counselor who told us about a beautiful place nearby where Lou could go. My mind silently added the missing words: to die. They were asking me to decide where Lou would spend his final days on earth, and I needed time to think. The counselor suggested I visit the hospice house.

Andrea and I drove over, and they were right. It was a lovely, calm place with a beautiful garden view out the window. Walking through it with Andrea helped prepare me for the decision I had to make.

They transferred Lou to the hospice house that afternoon, and the family started gathering. Christy came from Mississippi on Friday; Richard and Dianne came from Colorado on Sunday. Then on Sunday afternoon, Lou sat up in bed wide-awake and completely alert and said, "Harriet, I want you to take me home."

My first thought was panic. We couldn't do that. Hospice was the perfect place for him, with people to care for him and keep him comfortable.

"Honey," I said, "I'll have to talk to your doctors about that."

"No, don't talk to anybody," he insisted. "Please, Harriet, just take me home."

The children and I convened an emergency family meeting in the hallway. "I can't do this," I said. "How can we manage?"

"You're not doing this by yourself," Kevin said. "This is the family's situation, not yours."

Then he added, "Mom, I think you'll regret it if you don't take him home."

I hugged them all. We had twenty-four hours to transform our basement into a hospital room and get hospice care at home.

"Who can do that?" the children asked.

"My Sunday school class," I said.

Right away I called our teacher and said, "Roger, for a year you've been praying for us and asking what you can do to help, and there hasn't been anything. Well, now I need you."

An hour later I was home on the phone with hospice when the doorbell rang. There stood Roger and his wife, Sandra, and four other men from our class. "What can we do to help?" they asked.

They vacuumed, scrubbed, and moved furniture to make room, as the truck rolled up with the hospital bed. I had lined up around-the-clock caregivers, and the first arrived right before the ambulance that was bringing Lou. It was August 28, my birthday.

Dianne released me to attend to Lou by taking over the telephone. She contacted caregivers—hospice would only be there an hour or so a day. She dealt with the insurance company and all the red tape that piled up so fast it would have smothered us without her help.

The doctor had said we would probably have Lou for a week; God gave us a month. After the end of the first week, the parade of caregivers was confusing to Lou and to us. We needed one person around the clock. That's when we found Jinga, one of the most godly men I've ever known. Jinga never got frustrated, never got upset, never lost his patience. He bathed Lou and took care of him in a way that made Lou think he was doing everything for himself.

Lou was sick, but did not look or act like a man who was about to die. "Can you fix me some breakfast?" he always asked. So I cooked eggs and bacon and biscuits one day, pancakes the next. We all spent time alone with Lou reminiscing or just sitting quietly. None of the nightmarish predictions by the oncologist came to pass. Lou was talking and remembering to the end. He was even downloading songs, still using those iTunes, and singing with Johnny Cash or the Gaithers—"Because He Lives." Our children will tell you that month was one of the most cherished times of their lives.

Walking down the hall one night, I glanced in the bedroom door, and Christy, Andrea, and Kevin were all together laughing and enjoying each other. What an amazing gift, to be together as a family, the five of us.

Hospice had told us the signs to look for that would indicate the end was coming. On the fourth Monday, Lou didn't eat or drink all day, and by that night he stopped talking. He was shutting down. The hospice nurse prepared us that he could go at any time, definitely by Wednesday. I called Lou's sister, Linda, and invited her and her husband, Brian, to come out.

Then on Thursday morning Lou sat up again, alert. The first thing he asked was, "How's Kevin? Has he made it?"

When Kevin sold his graphic design business and came to work with me full time, it was a dream for me. I was going into my seventies, knowing I could pass the baton to Kevin. He had started at entry level and worked his way up, and shortly before Lou's final cancer diagnosis he had made a commitment to become a national marketing director. After Lou was diagnosed and given a year or less to live, Kevin considered delaying his push so he could devote that year to his father. But Lou wouldn't hear of it. He wanted to share in his son's success. He kept up with Kevin's progress through the months and continually offered his encouragement.

Close-out day, the last day to report sales, was the following Monday, and the new national marketing directors would be contacted afterward. It's a down-to-the-last-second push every year for the new NMDs. The Juice Plus corporate office knew our situation, however, and Tonya Oxley, the regional director, called Kevin on Thursday. "We don't want you to go into the weekend with this hanging over you," she said. "You've made it."

So Kevin was able to tell his dad that he had made national marketing director.

Sunrise

NOBODY WANTED me to be alone with Lou when he died. God had a better plan.

At four-thirty on Saturday morning, I went in to relieve Linda and told Jinga he could take a break. He went out to the porch. Cody was lying on the floor in the shadow of the bed. The nightlight was like a single candle in the room, pushing back the darkness and creating deep shadows.

Lou was not breathing as regularly as he had on Friday night, though he was still lying peacefully. I pulled the chair close to the bed and took his hand. Cody shifted and settled back down. I hummed some hymns and talked a little bit, reassuring Lou that I was with him and would always love him. The hospice nurses had told us that Lou could hear us and understand us even when he appeared to be sleeping.

Then Lou took a short breath through his mouth and exhaled, but didn't breathe again. The moment startled me, and I squeezed his hand. I couldn't believe that was it.

"Lou?" I said. "Honey, are you with me?"

Finally he breathed again, with considerable struggle. The hospice nurses had coached us on the signs. He was getting ready to leave, and I realized I wasn't ready. I needed to talk to somebody—Martie Hunter, my prayer partner for nearly fifty years. I looked at the clock: 6:15. So many mornings God had met me at this early hour in a morning quiet time as dawn began to break. The sky would turn from black to gray to light pink and yellow as the sun rose. Day after day God met me in the sunrise.

Martie would be awake in her own quiet time. I picked up the phone and dialed her number.

"Martie," I said when she answered, "there is nobody else I would call this early in the morning. Lou is really struggling with his breathing. He's ready. Would you pray with me that God would take him home?"

Then I listened to Martie pray the sweetest prayer for Lou to experience peace and God's loving embrace, and for the Lord to take him mercifully home.

I hung up the phone and took Lou's hand again as he rattled another breath, and I realized how dark the room still was. Yet the dawn was coming. I couldn't leave Lou's side. Not now. But I wanted to see the sunrise with Lou.

"Jinga?" I called. "Jinga, are you out there?"

He came, and I asked him to raise the blinds. "Open all of them," I said. "Lou's going home at sunrise!"

Jinga raised the blinds, and the dawn light immediately transformed the room from darkest night to beautiful morning. Cody stood up and looked around, and a wave of joy swept over me. I sat on the bed and cradled Lou in my arms. Cody jumped up and put his front paws on the bed, pushing as close to Lou as he could get, and then licking his arm.

"Honey," I said, "the sun is rising, and you're going home. Cody is right here with us too. You can go now, honey."

I glanced toward the window, and the sun was just rising through the trees. The children needed to come.

"Jinga," I said, "can you go tell the children it's time? Lou's going home now."

He left, and Cody and I were alone with Lou. This was no accident. The Lord was giving me this final moment with Lou cradled in my arms at sunrise, where He had met me on my darkest mornings. Then the Lord cradled me in His arms and poured out His light and hope.

Cody began to whine. "It's okay," I said. "Lou's going home now. He's ready."

Then Lou stopped breathing and he was gone. Christy, Andrea, and Kevin came in, and I stepped back so they could come forward. Cody did not move. He kept whining and licking and loving on Lou. Nobody tried to push him away.

The sun was shining brightly through the window. Lou was gone, and God was with us. A new day had dawned.

Hope in God's Faithfulness

GOD GAVE our family three Christmases with Lou at Promise Point. Each year we put up a tree by the front window that reached toward the vaulted ceiling, we hung lights that glowed brilliantly across the water, and we kept a fire burning. When you have nine grandchildren under your roof for a week at their favorite time of the year, you go all out.

The time between Thanksgiving and Lou's last Christmas with us, he bought all the grandchildren their own tackle boxes, along with the basics—hooks, weights, and bobbers. Then he studied his own tackle, especially the many, many lures he had bought over the years, and began dividing them up. His fishing gear was priceless to him, and he wanted his grandchildren to have it—not just to remember him, but to catch fish!

After our family had been restored, I began to see that Lou's favorite way of expressing his love was through gifts, often given secretly. We were at Promise Point one weekend when something hanging on the wall in the corner of the living room caught my eye. I walked over to see. It was a small, hand-painted, wooden plaque that read, "A fisherman lives here with the catch of his life."

For several seconds I just had to stand and look at it. Lou walked over, and I asked, "Where did this come from?"

He smiled and said, "I saw it, and it was true."

Three months after Lou died, we were celebrating another Christmas together, and I felt God leading me to tell the grandchildren our story. In our thirteen years back together, Lou and I had never told them about our years apart or how God had recreated love where there didn't seem to be any love left.

It was raining on the second day after Christmas, and all the children were inside. Brittany said Dylan and Tristan, their twins, were down for a nap (they were four years old), and it might be a good time to call everybody together.

"Give me fifteen minutes," I said, then I spent those minutes asking God to put words in my mouth so our other grandchildren, ages six to twenty-one, would grab hold of it. They needed to hear it in a way that would honor God and honor Lou.

"Tell it just like they're all second graders," I felt God saying, and that was a good thing. As a former second-grade teacher, that was a language I could speak. Then I went in and sat by the fire, and my family gathered around facing me.

I told them everything, from our courtship and marriage to Lou's leaving and my breakdown. I told them about God's supernatural re-creation of me physically, spiritually, and financially and His restoration of our marriage and our family. For an hour I talked, and at times we all cried together. Six-year-old Addison had a stack of sticky notes, and she never stopped writing.

As I finished, I said God was leading me to tell our story in a book. "But this isn't my story," I said. "This is our family's story, and I won't do it unless you agree that we should."

Aiden replied, "Nana, I've heard a lot of testimonies, but never this strong. You have to tell it." Then she added, "This is God's story and we have to tell it!"

Then Addison handed me her stack of sticky notes and hugged me. On each page she had written a word from the story, and on the top sheet she had written, "Nana's Book." In that moment, we knew we would tell our story. God's story.

We all held hands in a circle in front of the fire and the Christmas tree and thanked God for His faithfulness and for His miraculous restoration of our family. We prayed that when the whole world insists, "There is no hope," our story might reveal the hope that is in God's promises.

Let us hold fast the confession of our hope without wavering,
for He who promised is faithful.
—Hebrews 10:23

ACKNOWLEDGEMENTS

I am so thankful for our daughters, Christy and Andrea, who never lost hope that God would someday restore our family and were a constant source of encouragement, and our son, Kevin, who eagerly agreed that our story must be told and was willing to be vulnerable and share his painful journey to freedom.

Brittany, your loyalty and unconditional love for Kevin continue to inspire him to be the man God designed him to be. I thank God for the gift you are. I am grateful for the godly home the two of you have established.

Thank you, Barry and Jerry, for your prayers for our family through the years. You two are the ultimate "promise keepers" and I couldn't love you more.

I appreciate the encouragement and the prayers of my grandchildren during the time we have written our story. You are the joy of my life.

My children and I are forever grateful to the Barnes family for the gracious way they opened their home and their hearts to us. They continue to be faithful and loving friends.

When our daughter Christy was a baby, God sent me a godly mentor who would inspire and encourage me for years to come. Juda Kilpatrick has been a faithful friend and role model and has prayed for our family every day for more than forty years.

Thank you, Rusty and Joe Armstrong for the investment you have made over the years in Kevin's life. You treated him like a son during the time he lived and worked on your beautiful horse farm in New Mexico. Thank you, Rusty, for being my best friend from the time we were fourteen years old.

From the beginning of this project, my brother, Richard and his wife, Dianne, embraced my vision for the book, and throughout the process they have given me confidence and cheered me on.

Lou's sister, Linda Richards, helped in reconstructing Lou's growing up years. I'm grateful for her love and support.

Thank you to Dick Parker, my friend and partner in this project. Without his expertise, this book would not have been possible. Thank you, Dick, for patiently guiding me through the painful parts of our story, so that we could paint a picture of God's faithfulness and give hope to other families in crisis.

Jay Martin and the Juice Plus Company have provided me with a unique product and business model that has enabled me to thrive financially and personally. I am privileged to be a part of your vision . . . Inspiring Healthy Living Around the World! Thank you, Jay and Sandra, and each of my friends in our corporate office.

I deeply appreciate the commitment and loyalty of the national marketing directors on my extended Juice Plus team. Without your hard work, my success would not be possible. You are an inspiration and a joy to "do life" with. I am grateful for each and every person on our teams.

I would never have been able to manage the continued growth of my business or my personal finances without the expert advice and practical help of Tommy Turner, Dan Jones, and Malanda Kashani.

The Buckhead Boys, Lou's lifelong friends, demonstrated their love and concern for him all of his life, especially in his final days. Their loyalty inspired our entire family.

After Lou died, I was comforted by his faithful dog, Cody, who transferred all of his love and loyalty to me, becoming my constant companion. Recently, I had to say goodbye to our dear friend, as he slipped out of this world as peacefully as Lou had. I can't prove it, but I sure do like to think they are finally together again. I often picture them hiking through the heavens together, strong and full of life . . . and I smile.

Time and space will not allow me to mention the hundreds of faithful prayer partners who stood solidly with me during our journey. God heard each of your prayers and He graciously answered. You are a vital part of our story.

"Many will give thanks on our behalf for the gracious favor granted us in answer to your prayers" (2 Corinthians 1:11).